MIND
MAGIC

MIND MAGIC

TRICKS AND TIPS TO TRAIN YOUR BRAIN FOR A HAPPIER, MORE CONFIDENT YOU!

Keith Barry

by Nick Sheridan

An adaptation of Keith Barry's *Brain Hacks*

Gill Books

Gill Books
Hume Avenue
Park West
Dublin 12
www.gillbooks.ie

Gill Books is an imprint of M.H. Gill and Co.

This book is based on *Brain Hacks* by Keith Barry,
published by Gill Books in 2021.

978 07171 9985 3

Designed and illustrated by Luke Doyle
Edited by Ciara McNee
Proofread by Kerri Ward
Printed and bound in Great Britain by
CPI Group (UK) Ltd, Croydon, CR0 4YY
This book is typeset in Sofia Pro.

*The paper used in this book comes from the wood
pulp of sustainably managed forests.*

A CIP catalogue record for this book is available
from the British Library.

5 4 3 2 1

CONTENTS

INTRODUCTION

Hi!

Do you want to see a magic trick?

This book is **FULL** of them. And they have the power to **CHANGE YOUR LIFE!**

They're not the sort of magic tricks that will allow you to conjure ferocious white tigers from under your parents' bed.

And they're not the sort of tricks that will make your teacher's car turn into a huge, smelly block of cheese.

Thankfully for your parents and your teachers, these are different sorts of tricks.

And guess what? To perform these amazing feats, you don't even have to believe in magic.

You just have to believe in yourself. And I can show you how.

Allow me to introduce myself! My name is Keith Barry, and I'm a magician, as well as a father, a scientist, a mentalist, a hypnotist, an escapologist (yes, it's a thing), a mind coach and a **BRAIN HACKER!**

If you'll allow me, I can perform some mind magic on **YOU!**

I can help you to become more confident to try things you've never done before: Karate? Forming a rock band? Swimming with basking sharks?

I can teach you tricks that will help you to fix problems you encounter in everyday life, like standing up to someone at school who's making you feel bad.

I can help you to feel good, smash goals that you set yourself, bounce back when things go wrong (which they sometimes will) and make your life much more **MAGICAL!**

I've shown these tricks to sportspeople, from Olympians to international rugby players. I've used them on ordinary folks, and even **HOLLYWOOD CELEBRITIES!**

It doesn't matter who we are, where we come from, or what we want to achieve. We can all make small changes that make a **BIG DIFFERENCE** to our lives.

Maybe that's getting over a fear of dogs or becoming more confident at making new friends. Maybe it's calming down your mind when you get stressed out or upset, or maybe it's about standing up for yourself more in your everyday life.

Whatever you want to do, this book and the techniques inside it can help.

That's when the real magic happens.

HOW TO USE THIS BOOK

Each section includes stories from my own life. There are also times when you will be asked to put the book down for a while and **concentrate really hard** on what it is you want to achieve, and what the **best way** is to get to that goal.

To help you set some targets and to track your progress, I suggest that you keep a **JOURNAL.** This is like a diary, and it's the perfect place for you to write down your thoughts

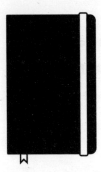

and feelings as you travel towards your goals. A good hardback copybook will do the job perfectly – just keep it **handy** and use it **regularly.** Like any skill, the more you write in your journal, the more helpful it will become.

It's probably best to read this book from beginning to end. But if you have a busy schedule of school, homework, sport, hobbies and sleep, that's no problem. It's written in a way that you can skip to the section that you feel you need the most.

At the end of each part, you will find some quick **ideas** and **exercises** that will help you to bring what you learn in this book into the **real** world.

MAGIC WORDS

These short phrases will help you to remember just how magical you already are. They will also help to build your confidence when you get into nerve-racking situations or are facing a new experience. They really are magic, because the more you tell yourselves these things, the more your brain begins to believe them. And that is a very powerful thing.

I NEED A VOLUNTEER ...

These exercises will encourage you to **put this book down** and bring what you've learned into **real life**. It could be writing a few sentences, doing some breathing exercises, completing a creative task or asking yourself some tricky questions.

CONJURING

These sections will ask you to conjure something in your mind. You might **imagine** something that will help to **calm you down,** or make you feel more **confident** and **comfortable** in your own skin. Your imagination is limitless, so you can expect to end up in some pretty **weird and wonderful** places. We'll talk more about your imagination, and how powerful it can be, shortly.

HEY PRESTO!

These are the short, fun-sized versions of all the advice you will find in each section. They come in the form of everyday **'brain hacks'**. Don't worry, no one is coming to **hack** at your brain (at least, not that I know of!). They're just simple reminders of all the great stuff you've been learning so far.

You might remember that earlier on I described myself as a 'mentalist'. That means that I perform awesome tricks with people's minds, including **mind-reading, predicting the future, sending messages straight to people's brains** and even **hypnosis!**

It might **SEEM** like what I'm doing is real-life magic, but here's a secret: **it's not!**

During my years as a magician, I have become an **EXPERT** on the big grey thing in between your ears: **your brain**. When I perform my tricks, I am using my understanding of people's brains to make it **APPEAR** like I'm magical.

And guess what: **you can do it too**! There are some pretty cool magic tricks within the pages of this book that you can use to **ASTONISH** your friends and family. Sometimes it helps to watch something as well as read about it. So to help you to perform these tricks, you can also watch a lesson of each one on my website: **www.keithbarry.com/brainhacks**, using the password **brainhacks21**.

Don't worry if this all seems a little daft when you're just starting off. **EVERYBODY** feels a little nervous trying something new for the first time. If you stick with these techniques and **PRACTISE** for at least ...

21
DAYS

OR

504
HOURS

OR

30,240
MINUTES

OR

1,184,400
SECONDS

Then these hacks have the power to make your life magical!

That brings us to the first magic power I'd like to tell you about. Believe it or not, we're all born with this magic power but most of us don't realise how **AMAZING** it is.

That power is called ... our **IMAGINATION.**

Let me show you how powerful your imagination can be.

Back in the 1960s, well before you were born (and me too, cheeky) a man called Alan Richardson had a sneaking suspicion that people's imaginations could be a little bit magical. He visited a team of basketball players and noted down how good they were at making shots at a basket.

So far, so good, right? Here's where the magic starts.

Alan then split the team into three groups.

The first group were told to practise their throwing for **ONE HOUR EVERY DAY.**

The second group were told to simply **IMAGINE** throwing the ball every day. Alan asked them to concentrate on making their imagination as vivid as possible. He wanted them to see the court and feel the weight of the ball in their hands. He asked them to hear the swoosh of the ball as it dropped neatly through the net.

The third group were told **NOT TO PLAY** basketball for a whole month.

At the end of the month, Alan got the team back together and recorded their accuracy again, just as he had done before.

The results were **astounding.**

The third group (who had done absolutely nothing) showed no signs of improvement. That makes sense – as we know, you won't get better at something if you don't practise.

The first group, who had practised for an hour every day, had improved – in fact, they scored around 24% more. For example, if a player had scored 16 baskets the first time around, one month later they scored 20 baskets.

Again, nothing very unusual about that – Alan expected the group that practised to get better at throwing, and that's exactly what happened.

But what about the second group? That's where the big surprise came.

That group had done nothing but **IMAGINE** themselves throwing the ball into the basket – but they had improved too! In fact, they had improved **ALMOST AS MUCH** as the group that had practised every day!

Had the group been secretly practising? Was it just pure luck? Was it a **magic trick?**

Nope, Alan realised, the truth was even more astounding: if we **IMAGINE** ourselves achieving something, then our brains begin to believe that we have already done it and believe we can do it again!

MICHAEL PHELPS is currently the most decorated Olympian **OF ALL TIME.** He has spoken countless times about the power of his **IMAGINATION** – how, the night before a race, he played a movie of his swim over and over again in his head – **IMAGINING** what it would be like to **WIN** again, to **SMASH** another world record.

'I VISUALISED TO THE POINT THAT
I KNEW EXACTLY WHAT I WANTED
TO DO: DIVE, GLIDE, STROKE, FLIP,
REACH THE WALL ... THEN SWIM
BACK AGAIN FOR AS MANY TIMES AS I
NEEDED TO FINISH THE RACE.'
MICHAEL PHELPS

Using the imagination in this way has become a very important part of achieving great things, no matter what they are. Amazing achievers like Johnny Sexton, Beyoncé, Jay-Z and even Albert Einstein used their imagination to trick their brains into feeling confident about reaching the targets they set for themselves.

And the best bit is: we're only just getting started ...

CHAPTER 1

FROM THE CRADLE TO THE STAGE

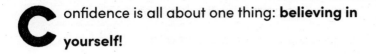

Confidence is all about one thing: **believing in yourself!**

It sounds easy, as if anyone can just **flick a switch** and suddenly become the most confident person in the world. Of course, it's much more difficult than that.

Every good magician knows that to perfect any trick, they need to practise. They need to repeat the trick over and over and **OVER AGAIN**, until eventually they can make it look like the smoothest and easiest thing in the world to perform. We need to practise confidence **EVERY SINGLE DAY** until we become confident without even thinking about it!

Think about someone you know who has confidence. It might be one of your best mates who has an **amazing** singing voice and loves to perform in front of people. It might be the **star striker** on your football team who is always encouraging other players to try harder. It could be your mam or your dad, or an older brother or sister. It could even be someone you've seen on the telly or at a concert.

Do you think they have **ALWAYS** been confident?

Well, here's a little secret: **nobody** is born with confidence. Babies don't come into this world full to the brim with confidence – just like they don't come into this world with a mute button.

In the same way that you are not born with the ability to read, ride a bike, do keepy-uppies or tap-dance while balancing a sword on your nose, you are not born with confidence.

Confidence is a skill that you pick up and learn as you go through life. Folks who don't have a lot of confidence have, unfortunately, had their skills, their looks or their thoughts **put down** and **knocked** time and time again by other people.

Everyone has had their confidence knocked at some point. Maybe it was a teacher who made us doubt that we could do something, or a coach who didn't give us the chance to prove ourselves. Maybe it was a classmate who said something nasty to us, or it could even have been a friend or a family member who didn't realise what they were doing.

The niggling thoughts that you sometimes have in your

mind have all been learned over time, e.g. **'I could never stand up in front of all those people and sing like he does'**, or **'I could never play midfield like she does'**.

Encounters with people who knock our confidence can end up reducing the amount of belief we have in ourselves overall: like the number of lives our character has in a video game.

In a video game, the more times we get **squashed** by a boss or **zapped** by a laser cannon, the more our health level will plummet. If it happens too many times, it might be **'GAME OVER'** and we're out.

Every nasty comment, every insult and every unkind joke directed at us will chip away at our confidence level, making us feel smaller and smaller every time.

If you're constantly being zapped by the idea that you can't do something, or that you're stupid or less important than somebody else, then eventually you're going to start believing it. And your video-game avatar's number of lives will be left at ZILCH.

I was lucky enough to have very supportive parents and a pretty nice childhood, but my confidence has sometimes taken a battering too!

Growing up, everything was pretty ... normal!

My primary school was just a short walk across the fields behind our back garden. My mum and I used to hop the ditch (avoiding nettles) every morning on the way to school. Along the journey, we would pass cattle and sheep, and in spring I often saw a calf or lamb being born before I sat down at my school desk!

Some people don't like school – but I found it pretty enjoyable and I had a lot of pals. We played outdoors together in all weather after school, maybe like you do with your friends.

Growing up, I had **two** main interests:

1. ANIMALS OF ALL **SHAPES** AND **SIZES**.

2. MAGIC.

When I was just five, I got a magic set for Christmas. My first ever trick went like this:

The magician places a ball under a cup, then lifts the cup to reveal that ...

GASP

... the ball has disappeared! The magician places the cup down, then raises it with a flourish to reveal ...

GASP

The ball is back!

It may not sound like much, but it amazed my parents and my sister, enough to encourage me to keep on performing tricks.

My parents saw how much fun I was having with that little magic set. Santa must have noticed too, because every year after that I would get a magic set for Christmas and my birthday (nowadays I mostly get socks, which is always a little disappointing).

As I got older and the tricks became more and more impressive, I grew to love **fooling** and **astounding** my audience: my family, my friends, classmates, teachers and even complete strangers!

Performing magic for friends and family was an amazing way to grow my confidence at a young age. My friends believed in the **magic**, and I began to believe in **myself**!

But then something happened that knocked my confidence **pretty hard**. I moved to a new school, which is often a really difficult thing to do. Maybe you've had to move school at some stage in your life, or have a mate who had to move to a new area and leave you behind. There are new **people** to meet, new **names** to recognise, new **teachers,** new **classrooms**, and new **rules** to follow ... it's a lot for a kid to take in!

I'll be totally honest with you: I found it **REALLY** difficult to fit in at my new school, and my confidence took a nosedive.

Most of the kids who went to Mount Sion lived near the school – so I was seen as an outsider. Not the **cool** sort of outsider that you see in films. Nope, I was the sort of outsider who got made fun of, got dead legs, bruised arms and the occasional glob of chewing gum in my hair **(eugh!).**

I tried changing things about myself to try to fit in (which is **never** a good idea, by the way), but nothing worked. I tried out a couple of different hobbies to try to make some new mates and get my confidence going in the right direction, but nothing stuck (apart from the chewing gum, **again: eugh!**).

One thing that I still loved through it all was **magic.**

I didn't ever really think I could make a career out of it, though, and had decided that instead I would grow up to be a vet. Like I mentioned earlier, I **ADORE** animals of all shapes and sizes and I spent the first summer of secondary school working with a local vet.

It may come as a **shock** to you, but rural Co. Waterford doesn't play host to many pythons, tarantulas or ~~hippopotomases hippopotamuses~~ hippopotami, so I spent a lot of time on farms. I'd come home covered in cow dung most days and my mother wouldn't let me into the house until I'd stripped off my work clothes. I must have **stunk!**

When I was 14, though, I got a taste of what it would be like to be a professional magician. I got paid to perform at a kids' party at a hotel in Waterford City. My uncle had got the job for me and I was **SUPER-excited**, and also **SUPER-nervous**. I came up with a routine and practised it over and over again at home. This could be my big break! My ticket to **stardom**!

If this was a movie, then I would tell you about how **amazing** the show was. How the kids were **dumbstruck** from start to finish, how they lifted me up on their shoulders and chanted my name. Then I would tell you how a **Hollywood agent** signed me up the very next day for a 100-year residency in **Las Vegas** and how we flew off on a private jet with my name on it and I lived **happily ever after**.

But this is a true story, **not** a movie. So I have to tell you what really happened.

If you have ever seen a gang of **ferocious** piranhas descend upon a piece of meat on the end of a hook, then you will probably be able to picture the scene. Though the piranhas would probably make less of a mess. Practising my tricks at home was one thing but performing them in front of **100 screaming kids** was a completely different ball game.

They basically **tore me apart** for an hour. Every trick I did they would scream **'It's up your sleeve'** or **'It's in your pocket!'** or whatever else they could throw at me. They even grabbed my props and pulled my pockets inside out! The whole way through my act, my hands would not stop shaking. I could actually feel and see them shaking but I couldn't stop them.

It. Was. Horrific. And it left my confidence at an all-time low. These kids weren't particularly nasty people – they were just young kids! But that afternoon, they chipped away at my wall of confidence – they were a big monster at the end of a video-game level who I just **couldn't** get past.

If those experiences happen again and again, you begin to doubt yourself. You might begin to withdraw into yourself a little, and not feel confident enough to express yourself and how you're feeling in case you seem silly or stupid, or not good enough. People who are **'shy'** often feel that way and it can be tough to try again – like it can be tough to go and pick up your controller from where you flung it the last time your health bar emptied and you were left at **GAME OVER.**

If people around you are constantly knocking your confidence, then the first thing to do is to use the word **'stop'**. It's a small word, but it's a very powerful one. Tell the person to 'stop' doing something that is whacking your confidence.

It's hard to do – it can lead to some difficult conversations with people, people who might be friends or classmates or even members of your own family.

Some people would rather avoid confrontation **AT ALL COSTS** and will continue to allow people to knock their confidence over and over again instead. But the truth is: the only people who like confrontation are bullies – and very often those same bullies don't realise they *are* bullies or the harm they are doing.

Now, I'm not calling the kids at the magic show 'bullies' – they were just little kids. But they behaved in a bullying way, and that first show left me running really low on confidence for a long time afterwards.

Slowly, over time, I realised that the best reaction to people who knock you, even after you tell them to **STOP**, is ...

Ready for it?

NO REACTION WHATSOEVER! GIVE THEM AND THEIR THOUGHTS **NO ENERGY.** NONE. **ZERO.** ZILCH.

Instead of allowing a bad comment to drain your confidence, just imagine yourself coming across a golden confidence-booster ring and rushing straight through it, sending your confidence **SOARING**. Then imagine yourself finding another ring and smashing into it, topping your confidence up to the maximum. Then have a smile and give yourself a pat on the back, because even though they don't know it, this person is actually *helping* you to **BUILD** your confidence, not flatten it.

When I told my granny about that first disastrous magic show with the piranha-children, she listened carefully. I told her that maybe I wasn't good enough to be a magician. She gave me some really great advice (which she was very good at doing).

She said: 'Well, that's life, Keith. Sometimes things don't go as well as you'd planned. We all find ourselves in situations where we feel out of our depth and that we don't deserve to be there. The thing you need to learn is that everybody feels like an imposter sometimes, just pretending to be good enough. The trick is to **never give up** and to keep doing the things you love until you realise you ARE good enough – or at least as good as anybody else.'

WE ARE ALL IMPOSTERS

We are **all** imposters.

Now, don't suddenly launch yourself at your teacher and try to pull off their mask to expose them as a **bank robber** or a 20-foot **man-eating MONSTER.** I'm not talking about *that* sort of imposter (though do take a very **close look** at your teacher, just to be safe).

An imposter can be anybody – it just means that someone is pretending to be something they're not. And doctors who study the human brain (while it's still inside your head) have  come up with a name for that feeling of low confidence.

That name is: **'imposter syndrome'.**

It's not a disease or anything like that, and you can't catch it if someone sneezes on you. 'Imposter syndrome' is when you feel like you don't belong in a certain situation, or that maybe you don't deserve to be there.

It's the feeling you get when you don't believe in yourself. It's as simple as that.

But something you may not know is that **EVERYONE** feels like an imposter sometimes. Everyone, at some point in their life, will think that they don't have what it takes to do something, or that they were given an opportunity by mistake, not because they earned it.

Maybe you've competed in a dance competition where the dancers who went before you were so **AMAZINGLY TALENTED** that you began to think there must have been a mix-up and you weren't supposed to be dancing alongside them. Someone with imposter syndrome might tell themselves, *I'm nowhere near as good as those other dancers.*

But you *did* deserve to be there. You just didn't **believe** you did.

Seven out of ten people **ON EARTH** have had that feeling at some point in their lives. Athletes, movie stars, singers, astronauts, firefighters, nuclear scientists, brain surgeons – even presidents! **Lady Gaga, Harry Styles, Serena Williams, Michelle Obama** ... all of these amazing people, at some point in their lives, felt the exact same way. Like they didn't deserve to be there. That they weren't good enough. Even though they really were, and really did deserve everything they'd worked so hard for.

Every single one of the celebrities and sportspeople that I have helped over the years had the same reaction when I revealed this simple fact to them. They always said, with a huge sigh of relief, **'So it's not just me!'** They are incredibly talented people, but they don't think they should be in the position that they're in. They're almost always waiting for somebody to expose them as an imposter.

This is good news for **you**! You should always remember that absolutely **everyone** has doubts about their looks, their talent, their intelligence and countless other things.

So, if you feel like an imposter before a hurling match or an audition, or when you're joining a new team or class, or even just meeting new people for the first time, remember this:

THOSE OTHER PEOPLE ARE, MORE THAN LIKELY, FEELING **EXACTLY** THE **SAME** WAY – OR HAVE DONE IN THE PAST.

My granny encouraged me to keep practising my magic, so I did what I was told and practised even harder. On a trip to Edinburgh with my school, I stumbled across the most magical place I had ever set foot in: a real-life **magic shop!**

There aren't many magic shops still around these days, but if you ever happen to come across one, I would strongly encourage you to take a peek inside. They're **amazing** places, and this one was no exception. I was blown away when I walked through the door and saw the number of tricks, props, illusions, gadgets and books inside. I spent most of my pocket money on stuff that produced 'smoke' from your fingertips when you rubbed them together, and also a couple of magic books.

When I got home, I put my head down and practised for hours every single day, trying to perfect the tricks inside the books. The books gave me some great new ideas, but magic is meant to be performed for an **audience** and I wanted to try them out in public. I was still a bit nervous after my first magic show and didn't really want to throw myself to the **piranhas** again. So I did a very smart thing and **asked for some advice** from my dad.

He told me: 'Keith, if you **practise, practise, practise,** put the work in and know you have done the best you possibly can to be ready, then you can be confident of success.'

PRACTICE MAKES PERMANENT

There is an old magician's saying that you should 'practise until your fingers bleed, then put on plasters and practise until the plaster wears off. Then you know you're ready.'

WAIT A MINUTE! Before you dash off to cover yourself in plasters, let me explain what this means.

To truly become the **best** you can be at anything – magic, singing, dancing, sword-swallowing – you have to practise until it becomes second nature to you. You should feel like you could almost do it in your sleep (though I wouldn't recommend **sword-swallowing** unless you're awake). Of course, you shouldn't practise so much it hurts (whatever that old magician says), but a little every day really will go a long way.

So my dad's piece of advice was a good one. I spent weeks and months with a deck of cards in my hands for up

to **EIGHT HOURS A DAY!** I spent that time repeating all the classic moves that every magician must know: shuffles, cuts, slices, lifts and tricks. I would hold the cards all day long, so much so that eventually they felt like a strange sort of extension of my arm.

Anyone who came into my sight, I would **pounce on** (not literally) and show them a card trick. I still do this to this very day, **so be warned:** if I happen to spot you in the street, I might show you a card trick. If you want to see one, then great! If not, then I hope you have a good pair of running shoes.

Sometimes I made mistakes: producing the wrong card from someone's ear, forgetting what to say or do next, or tearing apart a five euro note and being unable to put it back together (if you're reading this, sis, I'm sorry I haven't paid you back), but by making these mistakes in front of friends and family, it didn't feel like such a big deal. And I learned from them, so they wouldn't happen again, especially in front of an audience! It was **win-win!**

Practice is the key to defeating any challenge to your talents – it makes the risk of failure a lot smaller and allows you to **ENJOY** what you're doing a lot more. A lion-tamer who hasn't practised will probably find being locked up in a cage full of lions quite **stressful** – I know I would. But a lion-tamer who has practised their art for weeks, months or even years, will become more confident in their abilities to get along with the giant cats.

Making mistakes in front of people might sound as scary as being locked in a cage with lions, but you too can succeed if you practise. Try setting your mind to it and watch your confidence **SOAR**. Chess, football, skating, swimming, acting, even just speaking in front of a big group of people, giving a presentation to your class or making new pals. Practise whatever it is with your family, friends or someone that you trust. Make your mistakes in front of them so that you don't make them when the time comes for the real thing.

Hang on, you might say, how can I practise making new pals? How can I practise speaking in front of a big group of new people for the first time? And this is where we come to a very special word …

HELLO

A new classmate. A new teacher. A new friend. A new teammate.

You will meet thousands of new people in your life. **99.999%** of them will be lovely, but meeting someone for the first time can still make us feel a little anxious. Feeling confident every time you meet someone new is tough, but a few simple tips can help you feel a bit more prepared and make a **HUGE** difference.

In my life, it was **magic** that helped me. It was a great way to introduce myself to new people.

Here was my script:

(ENTER KEITH)

> KEITH
> Hello, how are you?

> NEW PERSON
> Hello, I'm grand. How are you?

KEITH

I'm great! My name is Keith. I'm a magician.
Do you wanna see something you'll remember
for the rest of your life?

NEW PERSON
Erm … OK!

(KEITH PERFORMS AN AMAZING TRICK AND THE
ROOM BURSTS INTO A HUGE ROUND OF APPLAUSE.
A HELICOPTER CRASHES THROUGH THE ROOF AND A
HOLLYWOOD AGENT JUMPS OUT, EXTENDING A HAND
TO A DUMBSTRUCK KEITH).

AGENT
Keith! Come with me to Hollywood, I've just
gotten word that you've won every magic
award on the planet simultaneously! We've
got to go and buy your tuxedo!

KEITH
WOOP WOOP!

Okay, so I might have gotten a **bit** carried away there,
but the first bit is true.

'Hello, my name is Keith. I'm a magician. Do you wanna
see something you'll remember for the rest of your life?'

At the end of this book, I'll show you a few of my favourite
tricks that I used to introduce myself.

But you don't need magic to have **confidence** walking into a room full of new people. Preparing a couple of sentences, facts or questions will help a lot too!

If you're going to a camogie camp over the summer, for example, then maybe you could prepare a couple of questions for your campmates. You could ask them who their favourite full forward is or if they've ever been to Croke Park or what their favourite position to play is. That's sure to get the conversation rolling, or **'break the ice'** as it's sometimes called. Once you've asked these questions and added your own opinions then **YOU'RE OFF!**

One of my first proper magic jobs was working in a local restaurant, walking around the tables and performing little tricks for the customers. I was delighted to get the job (that was a great confidence boost), but it also meant that every weekend I was going to have to walk up to complete strangers and appear confident. **GULP.**

I thought long and hard about another way of **'breaking the ice'** with all of these new people and finally settled on:

'Hi, I'm the wandering magician and I was **WANDERING** if you'd like to see some magic?'

DON'T GROAN! Yes, it's a very corny joke – like something my dad would tell – but most of the time it worked! It was incredible how **powerful** the simple act of introducing myself in a fun way could be. And that's the simple power of 'hello', a very magical word indeed.

It's a good thing I could earn a little money from doing magic at the weekends, because I soon found out that I probably wasn't **ever** going to be a vet! I scored pretty averagely on my exams when leaving secondary school – and to be a vet I needed much better grades.

So I plucked up my courage and told my parents that I wanted to be a full-time **magician** and **hypnotist** instead. Let's just say ... they weren't **DELIGHTED** by the idea. In fact, they were pretty set against it. In their minds I might as well have told them I wanted to be the **PRESIDENT OF THE UNITED STATES!** They knew that magic and hypnotism were talents of mine, but they saw them as hobbies – **NOT** as full-time jobs that could earn me money.

While magic had begun to earn me some pocket money, I still wasn't entirely convinced that hypnotism was **real** – mainly because I had never seen it work! I tried to hypnotise members of my family at home, but **nothing** seemed to stick: I couldn't get them to fall into a deep sleep and do whatever I wanted, however hard I tried!

Until **that** day in Irish class.

Trying to hypnotise my best mate, David, I sent him into a 'deep sleep' and commanded him to act like a chicken.

There was a pause, and **SUDDENLY** he leapt out of his chair, **clucking** and **pecking** around like a hen on one of the farmyards back home. As the class descended into chaos, I sat there as amazed as everyone else that my hypnotism had actually worked! He squawked, plucked, flapped and strutted around as my classmates laughed and my teacher bellowed at him to stop.

With a sudden **jolt**, the clucking stopped and David was back in the room, slumping into his seat, bewildered. He couldn't remember doing any of it, but he still got detention from the teacher.

That was the first moment I realised the true power of hypnosis.

I began to bring the art of hypnosis into my magic tricks, the excitement of this encounter inspiring me to spend even MORE time practising my tricks up in my bedroom. I spent **COUNTLESS HOURS** perfecting elaborate shuffling techniques, creating my persona of a confident and well-spoken magician with lightning-fast movements, invisible to the audience's untrained eyes.

The more and more I practised, the more I came to recognise the elements of tricks that worked, and the parts that didn't. I slowly but surely adapted the tricks to suit me, and they evolved into living and breathing beings that were entirely of my own making.

And they were working. Instead of awkward smiles from family friends when I messed up tricks, or giggles from my friends when things went wrong, I was nailing every single one. I was being clapped on the back and being begged to repeat amazing illusions. I was getting better, and **my confidence was growing** with every trick.

I was realising the true **POWER OF PRACTICE!**

CHAPTER 2
OPEN SESAME!

With my career as a vet out the window, I ended up studying chemistry in college. Unlike at secondary school, where I was seen as an outsider, I really enjoyed college. I made some great mates and **loved** Galway City where I was studying.

The **magic bug** had bitten me, though, and I still dreamed of being a professional magician and hypnotist. When I was 18, with the summer holidays stretching out in front of me, I got a summer job as a magician on the ferry from Rosslare in Wexford to Cherbourg in France.

I was part of a troupe of performers whose job it was to keep the passengers entertained. On board there were Irish dancers, comedians, singers ... and **me,** an 18-year-old magician. The family audiences weren't huge, but they were a lot bigger than I was used to and I could feel myself **trembling** every time I stepped out on the stage to perform.

Performing magic for little kids, as I've already mentioned, can be a really tough gig – and after a while I was beginning to **dread** performing. Whenever I would finish a trick, dozens of bored kids would **screech** at me that they knew how I did it. It was like being in that **bubbling tank of piranhas** all over again.

My confidence **buckled**, and eventually got so low that I would have to dash off-stage to be **SICK** half-way through the show. I got all the kids to shout the magic words **'WIZZY WIZZY WOO!'** over and over so that they couldn't hear me puking! So, if you're ever at a magic show and the magician tries to get you to shout **'WIZZY WIZZY WOO!'** loudly, you'll know what they're up to!

Just like the contents of my stomach, my confidence was being flushed out of me **pretty fast.** It felt like I was back where I started, being shouted at during my first-ever magic show and trying desperately to stop my hands from shaking.

One evening, as I stood in the wings waiting to go onstage, I found myself curling my toes as tight as they would go – my body was tensing up on me! I was also randomly mumbling to myself, something along the lines of, **'It's going to be OK, they're my best friends, they're my best friends ...'** over and over again, trying to calm myself down. Little did I know it, but I was in the middle of discovering my *own* **magic words.**

And these weren't silly phrases like 'WIZZY WIZZY WOO', which was just a jumble of nonsensical words that I used to PRETEND that I was a magical being. The magic

words that I discovered were much more powerful and had ENORMOUS power in the REAL WORLD.

MAGIC WORDS

Magic words, or **'affirmations'** as some folks call them, have been around for decades, and there's a reason why: they **WORK!**

To put it SUPER SIMPLY, 'MAGIC WORDS' are short phrases that we tell ourselves to trick our brain into feeling more confident than we are. Most of the world's top performers, from sports stars to movie stars, use magic words.

So, how do they work?

Well, we've already talked about how powerful our imagination can be, and magic words work in a very similar way. Just like the basketball experiment mentioned earlier, magic words work because our brains don't know the difference between **REAL LIFE** and a well-drawn **IMAGINARY world**. When we regularly repeat our magic words to ourselves, our brain begins to believe that they are **TRUE!**

How **amazing** is that?

Grab your journal, or turn to the back of this book, and take a moment to write down three short statements that feel special or important to you right now. These will be your first ever magic words that will help you when you're feeling anxious.

Don't make the statements too long, or you won't be able to remember them!

For example, if you are nervous or scared about what other people think of you, your magic words could be:

'I AM CONFIDENT AND BRAVE'

OR

'I DECIDE WHAT I THINK ABOUT MYSELF, NOT OTHER PEOPLE'.

Magic words, when repeated regularly enough, can help to trick your brain into believing you are **OVERFLOWING** with confidence.

From now on, every morning while you wash your face or brush your teeth, look straight into the mirror and repeat your magic words to yourself. I have little post-it notes stuck all over my house to remind me of mine wherever I go (though check with your parents before sticking notes all over the house, I don't want them to write me angry letters!).

Another magical sentence you may have heard of is: **'OPEN SESAME!'** Wizards use this phrase to get past enormous boulders and into magical caves, and with a little bit of mind magic, we can open doors of our own – doors that would usually have been shut in our faces.

Here's an example:

I was newly arrived in Dublin and one night I went into town with a mate. We walked past a very swanky looking place called 'The Kitchen' – with a red velvet rope and an **ENORMOUS** queue of people waiting to get inside. When my mate Damien saw the queue, his shoulders dropped, and he began to walk away. With my magic words ringing in my ears, I grabbed his arm and pulled him straight towards the **scary-looking** doorman blocking the entrance.

That was when I performed my first magic trick of the evening.

STAND LIKE A SUPERHERO

My dad used to say to me: 'Pull your shoulders back when you enter the room'. It was his way of saying, **'Look tall, be confident'**. The way you stand, or your 'posture', reveals a lot about the way you are feeling inside. If you're standing hunched over, with your head looking down at the floor, it can seem as if you want to take up as little space as possible. It can look like you're not confident.

And if you're not confident on the **outside,** you certainly won't be confident on the **inside.** Remember that our bodies as well as our brains can trick us into feeling stronger.

Standing with your legs apart and your hands on your hips, like a **superhero** about to go into battle, sends a signal to your brain that you're **FEELING** confident. Lots of politicians do this when they're about to give an important speech. It's called the 'power stance'. You should try it!

ACT THE PART

A very famous magician named Robert-Houdin once said: 'A magician is an actor **playing the part** of a magician'. (Fun fact: the most famous magician in history, Harry Houdini, loved Robert-Houdin so much that he STOLE his name and just added an 'i' to the end of it. Please don't follow his example and call yourself 'The Amazing Keithi!').

A great way to be confident at doing something is to pretend **you're an actor** who is playing the role of somebody who is good at whatever it is you want to be good at. If that means standing up in front of a class to read out your short story, or making yourself at home among a group of kids you've never met before, then pretending that you're playing the part of a confident person will help **HUGELY.**

When I was starting out as a magician, I was really just **PLAYING THE PART** of a magician until I felt confident enough to feel like I really **WAS** one.

When magic began to take me all over the world, and into rooms with **world-famous celebrities**, I calmed my nerves by imagining that I was playing someone else: a **cool, confident** person who belonged there.

For me, that person was Pierce Brosnan, the Irish actor who played James Bond in a few movies. Yours could be anyone famous you admire – **Daniel Craig, Dwayne 'The Rock' Johnson, Scarlett Johansson** or **Beyoncé** might be your modern-day equivalent.

Acting the part was another tool in my confidence kit, until I found that I didn't need to act anymore – I really **WAS** confident!

I NEED A VOLUNTEER ...

Put down this book and imagine a life-size hologram of the **super-confident** person of your choice appearing in front of you.

Watch how they walk, how they talk, how their posture looks.
Imagine yourself walking into that life-size hologram and transforming into that person. How does it make you feel?
Imagine the confidence of that person combining with yours.

Imagine all their confidence flowing into you and travelling through your body.

Feel yourself absorbing it all.

A phrase that is often used to describe someone that we admire and look up to is **'ROLE MODEL'.** Role models can be famous people, or someone who lives next door to you. It could be a family member, or an older person in our lives who we want to be like when we grow up.

Now, you don't need to go around actually pretending to be that person, walking and talking like them (that might **freak** your mates out a bit). But you should bring their confidence with you when you go out into the real world. When you meet new people, speak in front of a large group, or try new experiences, feel your role model's **confidence** inside you and let it **flow out** through your fingertips.

If you pull your shoulders back and hold your head high, repeat some magic words in your head and remember to make eye-contact with the person you're talking to, **magic things can happen.** Confidence can literally open doors, like the door of the venue I was trying to get into that night in Dublin.

The **scary** doorman blocked our way as we tried to walk in the door of the nightclub.

'Who are **you?**' he snapped.

It was time for me to perform some **magic.**

I pulled my shoulders back, looked him straight in the eye and imagined that I was playing the part of a confident person. I said some of my magic words to myself, then replied: **'I'm the celebrity magician!'**

There was a pause, which seemed to go on forever. His eyes drilled into mine. My mate Damien looked on, puzzled.

'Yeah, right!' the doorman scoffed. 'Do us a trick, then!'

I pulled out my deck of cards and performed a close-up card trick for him.

When the trick was over, he grabbed the microphone tucked into the lapel of his jacket and muttered a few words into it.

I stood there, watching him. Inside, I was **quivering** with nerves but on the outside I was calm, cool and super-confident.

Suddenly, the door swung open. Me and Damien were immediately welcomed inside and led straight to the VIP section.

OPEN SESAME!

CONJURE SOME CONFIDENCE

You will need your magic words for this conjuring, or you can use the ones I suggested earlier in the chapter.

'I AM CONFIDENT AND BRAVE'

OR

'I DECIDE WHAT I THINK ABOUT MYSELF, NOT OTHER PEOPLE'.

There's also a long list of magic words in Chapter 7 of this book that will help you if you get a bit stuck coming up with your own.

Sit or lie down somewhere quiet where you can hear yourself think. Close your eyes and imagine a purple light, like a floating spaceship, hovering above your head. We'll call this your **LIGHT OF RELAXATION.**

Feel the light float down to your feet, and imagine it softly washing over them, relaxing them. As you do this, repeat to yourself: 'My feet are relaxed, my feet are relaxed, my feet are relaxed.'

Now allow the light to spread through your feet to your legs, through your entire body, relaxing you as it goes.

Once your body is relaxed, pay close attention to your breathing. Breathe in deeply for a few seconds, hold the air in your lungs and then slowly release it. As you release the air, imagine that you're also breathing out all your worries. Then take another deep breath and repeat 20 times.

Now, imagine a gigantic cinema screen in front of you. On that screen is YOU, looking the most confident you've *ever been. Why do you appear so confident? Take a good look and see what it is that's making the difference.*

Think of your magic words and run them through your head over and over again as you stare at this perfectly confident version of yourself.

Now imagine yourself walking straight towards that cinema screen and MELTING into it. Once you've passed through the screen, imagine yourself TAKING OVER that confident version of yourself that you've been looking at.

FEEL the confidence flowing into your body, like a current of blue electricity. Notice every part of your body filling up with that beautiful blue confidence. Notice how differently you stand, speak and interact with the other characters who have come onscreen.

When you feel your confidence begin to bubble up inside you, allow the cinema screen to go dark and bring yourself back into the room where you're sitting or lying. Give your toes a good wiggle, then stretch out your arms and legs, waggling your fingers, and open your eyes.

This process is like learning to ride a bike. Sometimes you fall off it, and THAT'S OK! We might allow our minds to wander, or we might even fall asleep (guilty).

The most important thing is to try and try again. If you do become distracted, just bring your attention back to your breathing and the cinema screen.

Remember: practice makes permanent! If you practise this conjuring for two weeks, then I promise you will feel a huge boost in your confidence. And your mind will become more and more magical.

HEY PRESTO!

1. **Don't allow negative thoughts and negative people to drain your confidence. Negativity needs you to feed it for it to survive – so don't allow it to overpower you. Cut off its energy supply. Imagine it bouncing off you harmlessly. If someone keeps being negative towards you, tell them to stop. They might not have realised that they're having a negative effect on you!**

2. **Whenever you feel like an imposter in any situation, just remember that the other people**

there probably feel the exact same way, or have felt that way in the past.

3. Practise whatever you need to practise in front of friends and family, or in front of the mirror first. Make the mistakes there, not when it really matters!

4. Write down three short sentences that will be your magic words. Use these magic words to trick your mind into being more confident.

5. Pull your shoulders back, stand up straight and become a superhero before each nerve-racking experience.

6. If you don't feel comfortable making direct eye-contact, pick a point between the other person's eyebrows and speak to that spot. They'll think you're looking straight at them! Try it out!

7. Pretend you're an actor playing the part of a confident person. Pick someone who you believe is super-confident and play them, until you don't need to pretend anymore!

CHAPTER 3

THE CHAOS OF CREATIVITY

HOW TO THINK LIKE A MAGICIAN

Before you dive into this chapter, have a read of the puzzle below:

I saw my teacher fall off a fifty-foot ladder onto the tarmac at school today. She wasn't hurt.

How is that possible?

Have a **LONG, HARD** think about this. I won't give you the answer just yet, because I like to see people squirm **(mwahaha)**. When you've figured it out, or given up, read on ...

We've already mentioned how important our imaginations are when we're trying to make our mind a bit more magical.

When we use our imagination to create something, or solve a problem in an unexpected way, we are thinking like magicians. We are thinking **CREATIVELY.**

I meet folks all the time who say that they **WISH** they were creative. Often, what they really mean is that they're no good at 'the arts': painting, drawing, dancing, acting, Mongolian throat-singing, etc. But here's the thing:

YOU DON'T HAVE TO BE ARTY TO BE CREATIVE!

Have you ever measured something without using a ruler? Built a den? Hunted for treasure? Made a rope swing? Found your way somewhere using only a map? Made up a game to pass the time when you're bored? If the answer is yes, then you *are* creative.

Just like we need to practise being more confident, practising being creative keeps our imaginations **fizzing** and **popping** inside our heads. We are finding a way around things, or coming up with new ideas and solutions.

Think of creativity like a **huge set of dumbbells** that you might see a bodybuilder use in the gym. Except we're not trying to strengthen our biceps, we're trying to strengthen our **IMAGINATION** – and that's a **SUPER-IMPORTANT** part of having a magical mind. You can start by doing puzzles or wordsearches, jigsaws and even colouring books.

Just like confidence, creativity isn't something you're born with. That might surprise you, but it's true. **ALL OF US** are capable of creativity, and just like an energetic dog, if we feed and exercise this part of our brain regularly, it'll stay fit and healthy. Some people can be reluctant to try out creative activities because they don't feel creative enough. But not using their creativity muscles means that part of their brain weakens, just like any other muscle would if it's not exercised properly.

You're lucky! Kids are **ESPECIALLY** creative, much more so than adults. When you were a baby, and then a toddler, then a small child, you probably spent A **LOT** of time being creative: playing, drawing, making jigsaws, building things, colouring, painting, singing, the list goes on! You also would have had very few boundaries in your mind, and so found it much easier to play pretend.

Unfortunately, grown-ups allow other things to get in the way of creativity, so **CONGRATULATIONS!** You're already miles ahead of the grown-ups when it comes to your imagination!

HIGH FIVE!

THROW AWAY THE RULEBOOK

When I eventually decided that I wanted to follow my dream of being a professional magician, guess what most people did when I told them?

They laughed.

Not just little titters or chuckles, either. Big, bellowing laughs that made my eardrums **quiver** and my teeth **rattle** in my head. When I told my boss at the time, she laughed. When I told one of my old lecturers from college, he laughed. They didn't think I was serious! Surely magic wasn't a full-time career?!

The reason that they laughed was simple: they all had rules firmly etched in their brains that they thought couldn't be broken. There's no magic test you can do in school, there's no magic college you can apply for (I wish!). So they all assumed that someone could never do **MAGIC** as a **JOB.**

Kids have to follow **A LOT** of rules. When I was growing up, I had to follow them too!

'YOU **CAN'T** DO THAT!'

'YOU'RE **TOO YOUNG** TO DO THIS!'

'**DON'T** LEAVE THAT THERE!'

'NEVER STEAL GRANNY'S **FALSE TEETH** AGAIN!'

Parents, teachers, older siblings, babysitters, they all have rules that we MUST follow. And there's a good reason for most of them (Granny can't eat her Sunday roast without her teeth, after all). Rules allow everyone to live together in a happy and safe way. But when it comes to being **CREATIVE ...**

THROW AWAY THE RULEBOOK

Don't just throw it away. Throw it away, then **stamp** on it, **rip** out the pages, **flush** it down the loo. Being creative while following the rules is like trying to lick your elbow: impossible to do and completely pointless.

Let's go back to the puzzle at the beginning of this chapter.

I saw my the teacher fall off a fifty-foot ladder onto the tarmac in school today. She wasn't hurt.

How is that possible?

The answer is remarkably simple: **she fell off the bottom rung.**

Now, you may think this is unfair, that it's 'against the rules'. Reading the puzzle for the first time, you assumed that the teacher was standing on the top of the ladder when she fell. But nobody told you that – that's a restriction that you came up with yourself, a rule you told **YOURSELF** you had to follow.

This is a perfect example of how, when we're trying to be creative, we can impose our own rules on problems that have no rules.

Here's another puzzle for you:

A woman had two children that were born within the exact same minute, in the exact same hour, on the exact same day as each other of the exact same year, but they weren't twins.

How is that possible?

Give this some thought and when you've thought of a solution, or given up, read on ...

- - - - - - - - - - - - - - - - - - -

CREATE A CREATIVE ENVIRONMENT

- - - - - - - - - - - - - - - - - - -

Just like you can't scuba-dive in a bog, you can't be creative in a place that doesn't set your creative senses **TINGLING.**

First: **get rid of distractions**. Phones, TVs, computers, your Granny hammering at your door trying to get her false teeth back ... forget all about them and find a quiet, peaceful place where you have the time and space to think.

Once the ideas start coming, it can be hard to turn the creative tap off and you can begin to get **buried** under all of the fun things popping into your brain. For that reason, it's sensible to have somewhere to scribble them down: maybe a notebook, some post-it notes, the back of your English copybook, any white space will do. That way, when the ideas start coming **thick and fast,** you can **splat** them all down as quickly as you can.

Whatever your creative space looks like, and whatever size it is, make sure that it makes you feel calm. When I'm at home, I surround myself with books on all sorts of subjects which helps to inspire me and conjure up new ideas. I also use Lego, cardboard and Play-Doh to build little models of my ideas! You can build **anything**, from a character to an object in a book, to a scene that you're thinking of drawing. I also get some great ideas from watching movies and listening to music!

Posters and artwork are also super-useful when I need to be creative. Even a simple sheet of paper with some of your **magic words** written on it can help. You could stick a few onto the wall and let those messages sink into your brain!

I NEED A VOLUNTEER ...

Take a good long look at your creative space. How can you improve it?

What magic words can you put on the wall that will encourage you to be creative?
Is it bright enough? Is it too bright?
Can you see any object in the room that reminds you of a happy time, or something that you could write a story or a song about? Little objects like these can boost your creativity.
Can you see something striking out of the window, if you have one? A beautiful tree? A super-tall building? Is there anything you can see that conjures a story in your head, or calms you? If not, maybe you could stick some of your magic words post-it notes on the window to keep you focused.
Can you hear anything? Aeroplanes? Birds singing?
An ice cream van ...? Does that sound comfort you or distract you? If it's distracting, stick on some headphones or turn on some music.

Is there a television in the room, and is it on? If so, reach for that remote control and switch it off.

Decide on three things right now that you can change in your creative space to help the ideas begin to flow.

THE CHAOS CASE

Sometimes we all forget to tidy up, or just don't have time to do it. But **SCIENCE TELLS US** that if we try to be creative in an untidy space then our attention is drawn to the clutter and not to the **AWESOME** business of creating stuff.

The clutter competes for space in our brain, and **SQUEEZES** itself in.

It rudely **pushes** out the problem we're trying to solve and gets in the way of the flowing ideas. This makes us distracted, putting off tasks that we should be doing, and generally **stresses us out.**

Would we try to work on our biceps in a gym that was carpeted in rubbish, mouldy lunch boxes and chocolate wrappers? Probably **not,** so let's try to work on our imaginations in a tidy and clutter-free space.

Plus, how are you going to write down all your amazing ideas if you can't even find a pen and scrap of paper to put them on?

This is where your **CHAOS CASE** comes in.

Instead of scattering stuff all over your creative space – scraps of paper, puzzles, medals, birthday cards, magazines, comics, souvenirs – get yourself a box, bag, suitcase, bowl, ANYTHING that will play home to **all** those things. Label it your **'CHAOS CASE'** and fill it with all those things that could add to your creativity, maybe in a week's time, or maybe in a year's time.

Now and again, turn your chaos case **upside down** onto the floor and pick your way through it with an open mind. Creatively play with all the bits and bobs you find inside. You never know what your chaos case will inspire!

I had an idea one time for a trick where I would take a jumbled-up Rubik's Cube and upon throwing it in the air it would solve itself magically mid-air.

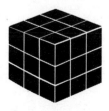

I couldn't find a way to pull the trick off and hummed and hawed over the problem for **AGES**. Finally, I went to my chaos case and emptied it out. After a few seconds, I noticed an elastic band around a deck cards and ...

WHAM!

I realised how I would do the trick!

The simple act of emptying out my chaos case sent rockets of creativity and inspiration firing off in my brain. It had the effect of sticking my hand in a pool of water and whirling it around, loosening all the sand and sediment from the bottom and bringing them up to the surface.

That is the power of the chaos case.

How did I use the elastic band to solve the problem? Of course, a magician **NEVER** reveals their tricks, but let's just say the elastic band ended up INSIDE the Rubik's Cube! 😉

Try to regularly clear out the chaos case and add new and interesting items that could inspire you to feel creative. That way, your creative space will stay tidy and your chaos case will constantly surprise you!

I NEED A VOLUNTEER ...

Get to work creating your very own chaos case!

Put in an interesting item that reminds you of something that happened to you long ago, a favourite book or comic, some Play-Doh, modelling clay or Lego – and three other things which you think could help the ideas to come running.

Now, back to our second puzzle:

A woman had two children who were born within the exact same minute, in the exact same hour, on the exact same day of the exact same year, but they weren't twins.

How is that possible?

The answer, once again, is very simple: the two children had another sibling – **they were triplets!**

If you didn't figure it out, then think about the rule that you imposed on yourself for no reason whatsoever.

You might have immediately assumed that there were only two children who were born together when no one mentioned that in the puzzle itself.

You might have heard the old phrase about thinking creatively: 'We need to think outside the box'. But what we actually need to remember is that there is **no box in the first place**.

This is fun, so here's another puzzle:

Two people were playing chess.
They both won.

How is that possible?

If you think you've figured it out,
or you're stumped, read on to find out more ...

Start with 'what if?'

To be **REALLY** creative, we need to fling our minds **WIDE OPEN**. Remember that there is **NO BOX**, and we have to be really careful not to create one for ourselves for no good reason!

Just like the word **'HELLO'** is a magic word, here are two more that have magical powers:

WHAT IF?

'What if' is a wonderful way to kickstart your imagination. Constantly asking yourself 'what if?' will lead you down some amazing creative paths that might never have appeared if you had just followed the boring old GPS.

When I was working on my magic show *Brain Hacker,* I wanted it to be a fun, mind-blowing show which used my imagination in really fun ways to come up with amazing illusions.

When I was walking down the street, I would spot someone across the road and ask myself:

'What if I could walk over to them and tell them the PIN for their bank card?'

This was a bonkers idea, but I followed the path that it was leading me down and began to ask more 'what if?' questions.

'What if they imagined their PIN floating in balloons over my head, one digit in each balloon. What if I could figure out their PIN from the way their eyes moved?'

'What if I could do it blindfolded?'

The method took a long time to get absolutely right, but by the time the curtain rose on the **Brain Hacker** show, I had perfected the illusion. I performed it onstage every night, guessing correctly **hundreds** of PIN numbers during the tour.

What if I could do an escape upside down 50 metres in the air?
What if I could do it on my TV show? What if I could do it while being restrained by a straitjacket?

That's exactly what ended up being aired on my RTÉ show, *The Keith Barry Experience*, a few years ago.

Both of these ideas came from random thoughts that walked into my brain.

How did I open the door to them? With the simple power of **'what if?'**.

I NEED A VOLUNTEER ...

Grab your journal and write down these questions. Then answer them with as much **CREATIVITY** as you can squeeze from your brain:

WHAT IF you wanted to make a coin disappear out of your hand in order to astound and astonish your mates?
WHAT IF you could use some sort of prop to achieve this?
WHAT IF you could distract your mates from paying attention to a certain part of the trick?
WHAT IF you could get one of your mates to secretly help you during the trick?

Start to think about three simple ways you could pull this trick off.

To help you start, I'll give you an idea: as I write this, I'm wearing a hoodie with a zip down the front. Using the classic magician's art of 'misdirection' to distract the audience from watching my hands too closely, I could move one hand up over the other quickly. While I'm doing that, I could flick the coin into my open hoodie, creating the illusion it has vanished.

Perhaps you could take a cloth or a piece of paper as

cover for a **SPLIT SECOND**. The more you think about it, the more options you will have.

Come up with at least three solutions for the disappearing coin trick and see what works best. When you decide on the best method, I want you to come up with a 'presentation' for that trick – a made-up story about how you will make the coin disappear! An example would be:

'I'm going to stop time, so that in a split-second I will be able to take the coin, walk to the shop, buy an ice-cream with it and eat it on the way home. I'll then snap my fingers, restart time and you'll think the coin has simply **DISAPPEARED!**'

Now write down three 'what if' questions that might help solve some sort of problem that you've encountered in your life.

For example, imagine your local dance class has had to close its doors because of a leaking roof. It won't be able to reopen for a few months. How could you creatively find a solution to that problem? Remember, just like in the puzzles, don't impose any rules on yourself that don't already exist!

WHAT IF the dance class was held in someone's garage every weekend, with everyone in the class taking a turn to host it? No one said the venue always has to be the same place!

WHAT IF the dance class was held in the local park? No one said the dancing had to be done inside, especially when the sun is shining!

WHAT IF your school could host the dance class in the assembly hall after school? No one said the class had to be on the weekend!

Before we finish this chapter, let's return to our final puzzle. Did you figure it out?

Two people were playing chess. They both won.

How is that possible?

The answer? **They were playing two different games, against two separate opponents!**

Who said they were playing **EACH OTHER?** Sounds like a rule that **YOU** made up!

CHAPTER 4

ROLL THE CREATIVITY DICE

PREPARE TO FAIL

You might have heard of a guy called Thomas Edison. He was a pretty big deal, mostly because he's the guy who invented a little thing called ... **THE LIGHT BULB.**

He didn't invent it on his **first** try, though. Or his **second**. Or his **third**. Do you want to guess how many failed attempts he had before he had his literal 'light bulb moment'?

1,000. It took him **1,000** tries before he made a light bulb that worked.

When Edison was asked by a journalist why he had made so many mistakes, he simply replied that he **DIDN'T** make a thousand mistakes, instead the lightbulb was **an invention that took 1,000 steps to make.**

Think about something that you've had to try really hard to get right. Learning a new chord on the guitar, nailing a difficult dance move, or even getting the right answer to a tough maths question at school.

Instead of thinking of the first few failures as **MISTAKES**, just remember Thomas Edison and think of each failure as **a step towards getting something right**.

When I was trying to perfect my PIN number illusion, I also got it wrong thousands of times. Now, I didn't want it to go wrong on the opening night of my magic show, so I had to make all my mistakes in front of friends and family first. I used them as **guinea pigs** so that I would get this fiendishly difficult trick right every time in front of a paying audience.

Failures and mistakes are **KEY** ingredients in the creativity recipe. They're as essential as flour when you're making a loaf of bread. As the wise saying goes: 'If you're not prepared to be wrong, you'll never come up with anything original.'

When you make a mistake or fail at something, remember that this is just part of the creative process and **NEVER GIVE UP**.

PIGGYBACKING

Back in the ninth century, an old man put on some fake wings and **jumped off a cliff.** He wasn't out of his mind – he was a Spanish inventor named Abbas ibn Firnas, trying to unlock the secret of how birds flew so beautifully through the air and attempting to do the same.

It didn't work, and he had a few bruises for quite some time afterwards (**ouch!**).

Although he might have failed, the work he did can be directly linked to modern-day aeronautics. When we check in for a flight and sit into our seats, hoping that the baby behind us will **stop screaming**, we are experiencing the results of Mr ibn Firnas's hard work. Without him, there wouldn't be planes, or jet engines, or rubbery aeroplane food!

You've had a piggyback at some time in your life. If you haven't, allow me to explain: it's when someone climbs up onto someone's back and gets a free ride to wherever they need to go. I don't get piggybacks much anymore because I'm a grown man, but if I'm super-tired after a long day I'll often wish I could get a piggyback just from my study to the kitchen!

When I talk about piggybacking on other people's inventions, I mean that it can be useful to rely on the knowledge developed by OTHER PEOPLE and then use that knowledge to create something new.

Most of the greatest inventions ever made are not created by one person: they are just the latest in a long line of inventors and thinkers improving – or piggybacking – on each other's concepts.

ABBAS IBN FIRNAS
MAKING WINGS FROM SILK
AND FEATHERS

LED TO

LEONARDO DA VINCI
DRAWING AEROPLANES
IN THE 1500S

LED TO

THE WRIGHT BROTHERS BUILDING THE FIRST AEROPLANE

LED TO

ELON MUSK SENDING SPACE ROCKETS INTO SPACE

While Thomas Edison may have got most of the credit for bringing electric light into ordinary people's homes, there were many other inventors who had already been working on similar ideas. What Edison did was begin to ask lots of **'what if'** questions as he improved inventions that already existed!

If you are trying to find a creative solution to a problem or puzzle that you're facing, you should follow Edison's example and look around at what's been done before. All problems are **opportunities** for **creative solutions**, and if you do enough research you are sure to find that somebody has solved a similar problem already.

ASK FOR HELP

One day, a kid was walking down a street and fell into a **deep hole.**

It was pitch-black down there, and the walls were so steep that he had no hope of climbing back out.

Looking up, he suddenly caught sight of his maths teacher walking past on the street above. He called out for help, and his maths teacher wrote down a long, complicated equation and threw it down to him. Then he walked on.

Next, his hurling coach went past. The kid shouted up for help, and his hurling coach tossed him down a hurl and sliotar and kept on walking.

Just then, one of his best mates walked past and the kid called up to him for help. His mate looked down in surprise, then took a deep breath and leapt down into the hole, landing beside him.

'What are you playing at?!' shouted the kid. 'Now we're *both* stuck down in this hole!'

His friend winked.

'Yeah,' he said, 'but I've fallen into this hole before and I know a way out!'

When you are trying to achieve something, or to find a creative solution to a difficult problem, asking for help from someone with the right experience who is willing to help is **ESSENTIAL**.

Brainstorming with these people, and listening carefully to their advice, will help to get your own creative ideas flowing. Sometimes these people are called **'mentors'**.

I have had many mentors in my life, and they have helped me to solve the most difficult, knotty problems – from designing magic tricks to much **BIGGER** conundrums.

A lot of people can be quite protective of their ideas and might even be reluctant to share them because they're not ready yet, but I think that's nonsense. Some people might be anxious that someone might **STEAL** their idea, but an idea will only ever be an idea if you don't **share** it with somebody. We should never keep our ideas locked up inside our heads because we're afraid someone might steal them.

And if they DO steal them? Well, it's a pity that some people might feel they're not creative enough to have amazing ideas of their own. It can be annoying if it happens, but because you've trained yourself to be a **CREATIVE** person, you can be sure that you'll have even more brilliant ideas **COMING OUT OF YOUR EARS** in no time. The person who stole your idea won't, which is a shame for them!

Now, we're bound to meet plenty of people in our lives who will be **MORE THAN HAPPY** to give us advice. The only problem is that some of them may not have a clue what they're talking about.

A brain surgeon would probably **NEVER** go to a butcher and ask for advice about a difficult operation they have coming up (at least, I would hope not). We should seek out friendly people who have **EXPERIENCE** in the problem that we're trying to solve and that we trust. So when we are trying to figure out a creative solution, we should look to creative people to help us.

No matter what I'm creating, I nearly always use another creative person to chat through what I'm doing and how to make my ideas better. Make an effort to surround yourself with wonderful creative people and make sure you help **THEM** out when they need **YOU** too!

SET DEADLINES

'Deadlines' might sound scary, but I promise you that they're one of the most useful tools in our creativity toolkit.

Whenever I want to create a new magic show, I always book a theatre, pick a name for the show (that's always a really fun bit), and begin selling tickets before I have even **THE SLIGHTEST IDEA** about what's going to be in it.

At that moment, there is no show. But I have a deadline and having that looming over me is a brilliant way to **FOCUS MY CREATIVITY** on that single project. I don't have a choice, I tell myself, I *HAVE* to be creative!

It works every time!

Sometimes deadlines can come out of nowhere and bonk you right over the head.

It was the grand opening night of my show *8 Deadly Sins*. Everything was ready ... **except** one thing.

The original plan was to do a big reveal at the end of the show, where the audience would be astounded when I unveiled the 'eighth deadly sin' on the stage of the Olympia Theatre in Dublin.

The words would be written on the floor of the stage in invisible ink, which would then be **DRAMATICALLY REVEALED** when a UV light was shone on it.

But ... there was a problem. When we shone the UV light onto the stage, **nothing showed up!**

The prickle of panic was beginning to run down my spine as we tried to figure out what was happening. We couldn't understand it! We were about **AN HOUR** away from opening the first show and we had suddenly lost our big reveal ending!

I brainstormed with the creative people around me, trying to find a solution to our problem. Then something dawned on us – maybe, just maybe, the light was bouncing off the stage like a tennis ball off a wall. How could we get the stage to soak up as much light as possible, allowing our secret message to be revealed?

The stage was squeaky clean – probably **TOO** clean. We decided that if we made it a bit dirtier, then the light might get absorbed into it and not fly off it. It was risky, but it was worth a shot.

With the clock ticking, I had to find some **dirt.** I ended up running outside and across the street to a nearby building site where I talked the astonished builders into giving me a bag full of dirt! I lugged it back to the theatre, up the steps and onto the stage, before emptying it all over the once-pristine floor.

With just minutes to go before the curtain went up, we flicked on the UV light and tried again. I let out a relieved sigh as the words finally appeared on the stage floor. We were off the hook!

Decide on a creative task that you want to accomplish and set a realistic deadline for when you want to accomplish it by.

It doesn't have to be an entire magic show or a 10,000-word story. You can start small and build from there.

Once you've decided on a **REALISTIC** deadline, write it down in your journal and stick to it.

- - - - - - - - - - - - - - - - -

DO SOMETHING DIFFERENT

- - - - - - - - - - - - - - - - -

You might have heard the phrase **'writer's block'**. That's basically when a writer feels like writing is impossible – they feel drained of all creative energy and are banging their heads off a brick wall.

This sort of block can happen to all creative people – when you fall down a hole and can't seem to find any way out. You might think that everything you create is boring or useless – and it ends up making you feel quite **bogged down** and **bad-tempered.**

It happens to me too, and it's happened to probably every creative person on the face of the planet. If you were pedalling your bike through a boggy swamp that was pulling you down further and further, you would probably decide to turn the bike around and change direction.

You can change your creative direction too. Imagine **slamming** on your bike's brakes, **wrenching** the front wheel in a new direction and **shooting** off down a totally different path.

How do you do that with your creativity? It's very simple, you just need to:

1. **Change your position.**
2. **Change what's around you.**
3. **Change what you're doing altogether.**

Taylor Swift makes **snow globes!** Tom Daley **knits!** Albert Einstein, one of the most creative geniuses in history (and owner of a very impressive moustache), used to interrupt his brainstorming sessions to **play the violin!** Winston Churchill took time out of leading Britain in the Second World War to **paint watercolours!**

Listening to music, reading a book, watching a movie, going for a walk, making some toast, can all change the wiring in your brain and give you a fresh angle on a problem. Exercise is particularly good at **boosting** your brain's creative thinking and problem-solving skills!

When I hit a creative swamp, and feel myself beginning to sink into it, I'll go for a walk outside and breathe in the fresh air.

The trick is to realise when you're getting into that creative swamp and change your direction in time. Don't keep trying to power through because you'll only sink deeper. And don't just stop pedalling and do nothing, because then you'll get nowhere. Always **CHANGE YOUR DIRECTION** and look for that inspiration somewhere else.

Even by changing the way your body is sitting can help. Stand up, march around the room, **do some jumping jacks!** All of these things can help to get you up and out of that creativity swamp.

DOODLE

You might have got into trouble for doodling at school – in fact, you may have even doodled on this book already! The good news is that when we've switched into our creative mode and are trying to come up with some creative solutions, doodling is a **MUST!**

In fact, why don't you do a spot of doodling right now? Grab a piece of paper, or, if this is your own book and not borrowed from a friend or the library, then there's some space to doodle right here!

That looks great! How did your mind feel?

When you doodle, you're allowing your brain to relax into a state of limitless creativity. Lines, circles, wobbles, faces, buildings appear out of nowhere, just as they should when we are training our imagination to be as free-flowing as possible.

I sometimes do a form of doodling called **'automatic writing'.**

I sit down with a piece of paper and a pen and allow the pen to rest gently on the centre of the page. I take some deep breaths and allow my mind to relax and float freely, then begin to draw while focusing on something creative that I want to achieve. I generally draw about 20 doodles in one sitting.

The fun part is always trying to decipher and decode what exactly the doodles mean afterwards. Sometimes it's impossible to make any sense of them, other times I can see things morphing into each other as my creativity blossoms.

 A doodled shape like the one printed here, could become some sort of **sea creature**, and then if I add **scales** it begins to

resemble an **alien.** That alien might end up holding a **Rubik's cube** and living under the ocean …

I now have a drawing of an underwater alien who has a burning ambition to become the **world's fastest Rubik's cube-solver!** They could become a book character, or a movie villain. Either way, just from a few scribbles on a page, I have the beginnings of a **story**!

Have a look at the shapes below. They may seem like boring squares and circles, but can you see a way to transform them into something MUCH more interesting? Grab a pencil and get drawing to make something magical – or if you've borrowed this book from a library, just copy them onto a blank sheet of paper and get to work!

I NEED A VOLUNTEER …

Use the purple light of relaxation we imagined earlier to calm yourself for around ten minutes, then think about what sort of idea you are trying to come up with. Focus hard on it.

Doodle for the next five minutes with your eyes closed, and simply allow your pencil to move wherever it wants to move.

When you've filled up four or five pages with doodles, open your eyes and take a closer look at them. If you don't discover anything useful then put the doodles into your chaos case for inspiration in the future!

ROLL THE CREATIVITY DICE

Here's a **SUPER** way to get your creative juices pumping until they're leaking out of your ears!

Grab your journal and write these six things down, then roll a dice five days in a row. On each day, complete the task beside the corresponding number:

PICK UP A RANDOM BOOK, GO
TO A RANDOM PAGE AND READ
THAT RANDOM PAGE FROM START
TO FINISH. CAN YOU THINK OF
A STORY THAT WOULD INCLUDE
A PERSON, PLACE OR THING
MENTIONED IN THAT BOOK? WHAT
MIGHT HAPPEN IN THAT STORY?
IT CAN BE AS WILD AND WACKY AS
YOU LIKE!

 TALK TO A CREATIVE PERSON
YOU KNOW AND ASK THEM A
QUESTION ABOUT AN IDEA YOU'VE
GOT, OR A PROBLEM YOU'RE
TRYING TO SOLVE.

 EMPTY YOUR CHAOS CASE AND
PLAY WITH THE CONTENTS.

 ASK AS MANY PEOPLE AS YOU
CAN IF THEY KNOW ANY JOKES. IF
THEY TELL YOU ONE, THEN TELL
THEM ONE OF YOUR OWN.
LISTEN TO A PIECE OF MUSIC THAT

YOU LOVE AND IMAGINE WHAT KIND OF MOVIE IT MIGHT WORK FOR AS A SOUNDTRACK.

 GO FOR A SHORT WALK, AND TRY TO SPOT THREE THINGS THAT INSPIRE YOU.

These six tasks are all designed to **BOOST YOUR CREATIVITY**, and, of course, you can use your imagination all over again to come up with new lists every week!

REMEMBER!

ANYONE can be creative, but you have to **BELIEVE** that you have the ability to see the world differently. I know you do.

Allow your imagination to take centre stage, let it fly and hang onto it as tightly as you can. Ask yourself magical questions, and soon you'll be thinking like a magician!

1. When you're coming up with creative ideas and solutions, don't limit yourself with rules that don't exist.

2. Change three things about the space around you today to help kick-start your creative thinking.

3. Keep clutter out of sight, allowing your imagination to run free. Use a chaos case to store interesting items and dump everything out every now and then to look for inspiration.

4. ALWAYS ask yourself magical 'what if?' questions. Every mistake or failure is a step on the journey towards something brilliant. If you're not ready to be wrong, you'll never come up with anything original!

5. Share the beginnings of an idea with other creative people. Ask for help when you need it and give it to others when it's needed.

6. Give yourself a deadline for a task. That way you're MUCH more likely to focus your attention

on the problem you're trying to solve, or an idea you're trying to conjure.

7. Change your position, the space around you, or what you're doing to find a new direction. If you're feeling bogged down in the creative swamp, slam on the brakes and head down a different path.

8. Doodle as much as you can to get the creative juices flowing. Doodle in your journal and take a close look at what you come up with. If it doesn't kick-start your creativity right away, then pop it in your chaos case for later.

9. Pick six different things to inspire creativity and roll a dice each day to see which one you will use.

CONJURE SOME CREATIVITY

Use your light of relaxation and breathing exercises to enter your relaxation zone.

Now, imagine you are in an empty room, with every surface painted a bright, brilliant white. Out the window you can see rolling green hills under a cheery yellow sun. This is your Room of Creativity, and in the corner sits a table covered with coloured markers, brushes, pencils and paint pots of every colour you can imagine.

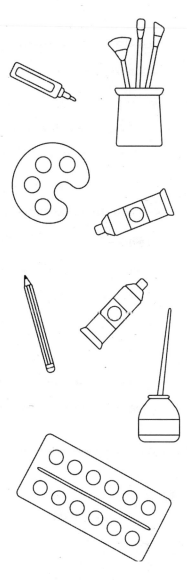

Think about something in your life that asks you to be **CREATIVE**. That could be a story you're writing, a picture you'd like to draw or paint, a dance move that you're practising, a box of Lego that you want to build something out of, growing your own plants in your kitchen, a boring bedroom wall that you want to make look **AWESOME**. It could be a den you want to build, a tricky problem in a video game that you want to solve – it really could be **ANYTHING**.

Think of all the possibilities, inspirations and solutions that you can come up with. Visualise yourself grabbing the markers from the table and scribbling ideas onto the walls. Don't hesitate, don't pause to think. Just follow your ideas and see where they take you.

Sometimes the ideas will come at lightning-speed, other times they'll be a bit slower to turn up. Don't try to hurry them along, let them come in their own time. The more you practise this exercise, the faster the answers will appear.

When the ideas begin to dry up, look around the Room of Creativity and focus on what you've written there. Take it all in, then imagine wiping the walls clean again. Bring yourself back into the room that you're sitting or lying in. Begin to bring the feeling back into your toes, your legs, your whole body and then open your eyes.

Grab your journal and write down as many ideas as you can remember. Pick one and play around with it like you would with something from your chaos case. Could

the den be spaceship-themed? Instead of painting your bedroom wall with a boring colour, maybe you could cover it with lots of colourful photos? If you don't have a garden to plant flowers in, could you cut a milk carton in half and plant some seeds in there? See if this idea might help you in whatever creative project you're working on.

CHAPTER 5

THE TARGET FORMULA

Let's **zip** right back in time to when I was around your age, growing up in rural Waterford.

Not to sound like an **old fossil** who's just been dug up after centuries underground, but when I was growing up we didn't have much to keep us entertained – **no laptops, no iPads, no smartphones.** Deep in the dark nights of winter, my sister and I wo finish our homework and dash nex door to our grandparents' house, where we would engage in **ferociously** competitive games of darts.

Thankfully no one ever **lost an eye**! My sister and I weren't great players, so we were allowed to stand a little bit closer to the dartboard, which was hung on the back of my granny's kitchen door. The only target we hoped to hit was the dartboard itself, and not the door – the bullseye was only a pipe dream for us!

Random fact: my mam had been trained in the art of darts all her life by my granny, so she was a bit of a darts supremo. In fact, she got **SO** good at it that she ended up representing the province of Munster in a **darts competition!**

Anyway, I always loved going over to my granny's and hammering darts into her poor kitchen door. But it's only as I've grown up that I've begun to realise how much those games taught me about hitting targets.

My mother would always tell me, 'You're not going to get what you want if you don't aim for it!' as I tossed another dart miles wide of the board and **narrowly missed my grandad's head.** She was telling me that there was no point in just aimlessly throwing darts at the board. If I needed to hit a specific spot to win a game, I had to **FOCUS** on that one spot. I would focus until it seemed like there was nothing else in the world but that **ONE SPOT.**

As I've got older, I've realised that you can say the exact same thing about anything you want to achieve, **big** OR **small.**

I've set plenty of targets in my life, and maybe you have too!

Learn a certain piece of music on an instrument? Get on to the basketball team? Save up your pocket money to buy something special?

These are all targets that are achievable, but only if we decide that we are going to aim for them and **FOCUS** on that aim.

All the targets I've ever missed are the ones where I got distracted, lost my focus or gave up too soon.

So, what is a target?

Simply put, a target is a clearly defined **OBJECTIVE** that you want to accomplish before that **DEADLINE** that we spoke about earlier.

When I say, 'clearly defined', I mean that there must be an easy way of telling whether you actually hit the target or not.

Let's say there's a big wall standing in front of us, painted red all over. I give you a dart and ask you to hit an **EXACT** spot on the wall – not an inch to the left or right. I point at the spot vaguely and tell you to go ahead and throw.

When your dart hits the wall, we are going to have quite a bit of trouble figuring out if you hit the spot or not.

That's because I've asked you to hit one red spot hidden amongst countless other identical red spots.

What I **SHOULD** have done is dip a paintbrush in a bucket of **WHITE** paint and dab a little spot onto the wall. That way, when you throw your dart, we will both be in **ZERO DOUBT WHATSOEVER** about whether you've hit it or not.

And that is a **CLEARLY DEFINED TARGET** – the only sort of target that we should set for ourselves.

Not: 'I really want to be able to play the guitar by next year.'

But: 'I really want to be able to play the chords of G, D, Em and A on the guitar by the time I go back to school after the summer holidays.'

Clearly defined targets work really well because they force us to set **DEADLINES,** and as I've already mentioned, deadlines are super-important.

Once the target is clearly seen in our minds, then we can map out the route that we will take towards reaching it, just like a GPS or sat-nav will break down a journey into lots of little steps. If we want ice cream, we don't expect to leap out of bed and land in an ice-cream shop – we get out of bed, dash out the front door, walk down the street and through the front door of the shop. Each journey towards a target is just a series of little targets, one after the other.

With the example of learning the guitar, having a clear target like being able to play four chords by the time you go back to school would help you to map out your journey:

'I'll spend the next two weeks working on the chord of G, then add in the chord of D for two weeks and then I'll add Em. Then in two weeks' time I'll practise bringing all four together.'

Just like a heat-seeking **MISSILE**, you will find your way over, under, around and through anything that stands in your way.

Sometimes in boring maths questions, we're told to follow a 'formula' to get to the answer. A formula just means a set pattern of moves to tackle a problem.

If you have to press a certain set of buttons to get a video-game character to execute an awesome move, then you are following a formula. If your football coach comes up with a passing formation to get the ball to your striker to score a screamer of a goal, then the team is following a formula.

My **TARGETS** formula is just like that – and I've used it to turn my passion for magic into a career, to get my own TV shows in Ireland and America, to be a star performer with my own magic show in **LAS VEGAS**, and lots more successes in my life. Now, I'm going to share it with you.

TARGETS STANDS FOR:

TAKE AIM!

ACTION!

RECORD IT!

GAME TIME!

EXPECT PROBLEMS!

TEAM UP!

SMASHED IT!

TAKE AIM!

If you don't take proper aim at something, then you'll never hit what you really want to achieve. Getting 100% in an Irish test, winning a school table quiz, memorising every flag of every country in the world – these are all targets that have a clearly-defined bullseye. Without that, you'll miss your targets and maybe even lose your darts. You'll get fed up playing the game and settle for something less exciting instead.

When I first started playing darts, my first target was simply to **HIT THE BOARD**, and not the picture of the Pope on my granny's kitchen wall (sorry again, Granny).

When I was able to hit the board with each throw, I took a few steps back and tried to hit the highest-scoring spot on the board (which, if you've ever played darts, is actually a triple 20, and **NOT** the bullseye!).

After a lot of time and practice (there's that P word again), I was finally able to hit any number I wanted, most of the time.

If you want to hit a target, then the process will be the exact same for you.

There are a few different types of targets though, and it's useful to know which type we're working with. We can decide the type of target we mean by thinking about the **DEADLINE** that we're going to set ourselves for each one.

Here are four different targets that you might have if you love athletics and want to improve:

SHORT-TERM TARGET: GO FOR A JOG AROUND THE SPORTS PITCH TODAY.

MEDIUM-TERM TARGET: GET PICKED FOR YOUR ATHLETICS CLUB'S FIRST TEAM FOR THE NEXT COUNTY HEATS.

LONG-TERM TARGET: WIN A PLACE ON THE PODIUM AT A NATIONAL COMPETITION WITHIN 12 MONTHS.

MAGICAL TARGET: WIN A GOLD MEDAL FOR IRELAND AT THE OLYMPICS.

You will notice that each of my targets leads on to the next one – they're like stepping stones towards my big **MAGICAL TARGET.**

MAGICAL TARGETS are the ones that are so crazy, so wild and **FAR-FETCHED** that usually you would never consider them as targets in the first place. Most people miss out on having these targets in their life – but they are just as important as all the other targets that you set for yourself.

Everyone needs zany targets too – like doing a parachute jump, starring in a movie, running a marathon dressed like a chicken, winning an Olympic gold medal – whatever you choose. They can be as **MAGICAL** as you like.

What's **MY** magical target? I want to climb Mount Kilimanjaro, one of the highest mountains in the world, in my underpants!

WHY WOULD I WANT TO DO THAT? Well, it's an adventure! And we all need a little bit more **MAGIC** in our lives!

Grab your journal and let's set down some **TARGETS.**

Draw four circles inside each other, like the dartboard below.

In the outer ring of the dartboard write down **SIX SHORT-TERM TARGETS.**

Moving closer to the bullseye, write down **THREE MEDIUM-TERM TARGETS.**

In the ring surrounding the bullseye, write down **ONE LONG-TERM TARGET.**

Finally, in the bullseye, write down your **MAGICAL TARGET.**

Add some doodles that represent your targets. Now that you've **DEFINED** your targets, you can start throwing your darts.

ACTION!

OK, we've decided what our targets are.

WHAT NOW?

Well, now we can take the first step towards **WHACKING** our dart into that target.

If we do nothing, nothing will happen.

If we do something small, something small will happen.

If we do something half-heartedly, only half a thing will happen.

What we've got to do is ...

TAKE MASSIVE ACTION!

Think of that heat-seeking missile, blasting itself towards a target. It is huge and unstoppable, and all its energy is focused on **SMASHING** into its target with **TEETH-RATTLING FORCE.**

That's the energy we need to release when we take action towards hitting our target.

If I decide I want to win a gold medal at the Olympics, it's not enough for me to ask for a new pair of runners for Christmas and then let them sit in a box under my bed. It's not enough for me to go for a short walk every weekend.

I need to take **MASSIVE ACTION**, and that's working hard whenever I can to get quicker at running long distances. I need to **BLAST** myself towards that target.

A few years ago, I set myself the target of appearing on one of the biggest TV chat shows in the United States, watched by around **4 MILLION PEOPLE**. No big deal, right?!

I asked my agent for advice. He said: 'Well, Keith, that's going to be hard. There are **THOUSANDS** of people trying to get on that show every day.'

CHALLENGE **ACCEPTED.**

It was time for some **MASSIVE ACTION.**

Starting from zero, I Googled producers who worked on the show and sent out **30 EMAILS**. Then I sat back and waited.

NOTHING.

I looked up phone numbers for the show and called every single producer.

NOTHING.

I sent out **ANOTHER** 30 emails and made 20 **MORE** calls.

STILL NOTHING. It wasn't going well.

But I had decided on my **TARGET** and I was laser-focused on hitting it. I do that with **EVERY TARGET** I set myself in life. I told everyone who would listen to me that I was going to be on this TV show before the end of the year. I promised myself a reward if I got on it!

In the end, it took me **92 EMAILS** and **46 PHONE CALLS**, but I did get on that TV show and it was **AMAZING!**

The only reason I hit that target was because I took **MASSIVE ACTION** and continued to take that action until I smashed it.

Some folks take baby steps towards a target, and sometimes that's got to be done. Remember though: *the smaller the steps you take, the longer your journey is going to be*.

The perfect time to begin working towards your target is ...

RIGHT
NOW!

To be a world-famous magician, you've got to practise right now.

To be a rockstar, you've got to learn those guitar chords right now.

To hit your target, you've got to take **MASSIVE ACTION** ... right now!

Decide what **MASSIVE ACTION** looks like for you.

Are you ready to put in the **EFFORT** and **DEDICATION** needed to smash your target?

How are you going to do that?

How much **TIME** are you willing to put into **SMASHING** your target?

- - - - - - - - - - - - - - - - - -

RECORD IT!

- - - - - - - - - - - - - - - - - -

If you've decided that you want to be able to do 100 keepy-uppies in one go, never letting the ball drop, how will you know if you're **making progress** or not as the weeks pass by?

You can **RECORD** your progress towards your target. Maybe you'll start off by doing three keepy-uppies, then the week after you'll be able to do ten, then the week after that you'll be able to do fifteen.

If a week passes and you find you can still only do 15, then you should ask yourself why, and change whatever it is that's holding you back. You couldn't have made that change if you hadn't **RECORDED** your progress and realised that something wasn't right!

If you find that the air is leaking out of your football, you can pump it up. If you think that you haven't given yourself enough time to hit your target, then you can move your **DEADLINE** a little further into the future. If, however, you find that you're able to do more keepy-uppies than you expected, then you can move your **DEADLINE** a little closer and move on to the next target once you've smashed that one – maybe 200 keepy-uppies?

 If you want to be able to run for half an hour without stopping, keep a note of how long you can run for each time you head out for a jog.

If you want to read 10 books over the summer holidays, keep a note of how many books you've got through as the weeks go by.

If you find that you're off-track, and likely to miss your deadline, then either adjust what you're doing or adjust your deadline slightly.

Discuss your progress (or lack of progress) with someone you trust. They may be able to offer advice or encouragement. That way, you'll have constant reminders of what your target is and how close you are to **SMASHING** it.

As well as that, **RECORDING** your progress can make you feel really good. Who doesn't love ticking something off a list, or looking at the pile of books they've read? The sense of satisfaction and achievement you'll get when you are progressing well is **AMAZING**.

- - - - - - - - - - - - - - - -

GAME ON!

- - - - - - - - - - - - - - - -

Adding a bit of competition is another great way to **SMASH** your target. This competition isn't against someone else, it's actually with **YOURSELF.**

Don't worry, you don't need to clone yourself and run the risk of releasing an evil twin into the world. You just need to promise yourself a little **REWARD** when you smash a short-term, medium-term or long-term target.

There's a reason people offer **REWARDS** for information on crooks on the run – they work!

Some targets take a lot of hard work to hit, so making a game out of your progress towards them will help to keep you **SUPER-FOCUSED** and **EXCITED** about the next reward.

A WARNING! Try to make sure that the reward doesn't make it harder for you to hit the target you're aiming at.

A cowboy on the run from the law in the mountains probably wouldn't celebrate evading a sheriff by throwing a huge party with balloons, streamers and a hog-roast. If he did, the sheriff would know exactly where he was and would end up dragging him back to face justice.

An athlete preparing to run ten marathons in a row **probably** wouldn't celebrate running five in a row by taking a break from running for a month. If they did, they would probably end up right back where they started.

And someone who wanted to save up their pocket money to buy a video game **probably** wouldn't celebrate hitting half their target by buying a different video game.

My passion is magic, of course, so I will often reward myself with a new trick or illusion whenever I **SMASH** one of my targets. It's a really fun way to keep your interest in what you're doing.

The idea of **'Game on!'** is all built around a little chemical in your brain called **'dopamine'.** Your brain releases dopamine all around your body when you experience something good.

If you've ever scored a winning goal in the dying moments of a game, the buzz that you feel is the dopamine **WHIZZING** through your body. If you've ever got a super-tricky maths question right the first time, then you'll have felt the fizzing sensation that the dopamine brings.

One thing that makes our dopamine levels **ROCKET** is when we receive a reward for doing something. That's why your mam or dad will often promise to give you a reward if you do something boring, like taking the bins out, feeding the cat or making your bed.

Decide now on some rewards that you are willing to give yourself if you reach certain checkpoints along the journey to **SMASHING** your targets. Write down these rewards in your journal so you can constantly remind yourself of them.

- - - - - - - - - - - - - - - - - - - -

EXPECT PROBLEMS!

- - - - - - - - - - - - - - - - - - - -

The next step towards smashing your target is to **expect problems.**

'**What?!**' I hear you shout, opening the window and getting ready to fling this book out of it. 'Why should I start this process with such a bad attitude?! Expecting problems from the very start sounds very **NEGATIVE** to me, Keith!'

Please, close the window and sit back down for a second. **Let me explain.**

Expecting problems isn't negative thinking – it's just being prepared for them if they crop up.

Beekeepers don't collect honey from their bees in their **underpants.** They wear a protective suit and face-mask **IN CASE** the bees get a bit tetchy and try to sting them.

And camogie players don't run out on the pitch without a helmet, **JUST IN CASE** an over-enthusiastic full back takes a wild swing and **whacks** them on the forehead.

If the bees **DO** wake up in a bad mood and try to sting the beekeeper, they'll be protected. If that over-enthusiastic full back **DOES** take a wild swing at our camogie player, they'll get a bonk on the helmet and not on the head.

If you expect obstacles and problems and properly prepare for them, then they'll be **MUCH** easier to overcome.

By the time I perform an escape while chained and

padlocked in a container full of water, I will already have spent tons of time thinking over the possible problems I might face. The locks might not work! The chains might get rusty in the water and stick! The water might be too cold and I might go into shock!

These all sound like scary things that could happen, but we don't need to be worried about problems. Most of them will **NEVER HAPPEN.** But if we're prepared for them, then we'll simply **DEAL WITH IT** in the way that we've planned and move forwards.

If we're trying to win an Olympic gold medal in athletics for Ireland, then a potential problem could be tripping over and falling hard on the ground, injuring ourselves and being out of action for weeks.

We can prepare for that possible problem by only running on soft ground, like the grassy area of a park or our local pitch. That way, if we **DO** end up tripping over, we're much less likely to injure ourselves. Problem **SEEN** and problem **SOLVED!**

I NEED A VOLUNTEER ...

Grab your journal and think about the targets that you're aiming for right now.

Try to think about as many obstacles as you can, that could get in the way of you smashing that target. What might go wrong?

Write down three possible solutions to every obstacle you can think of.

Remember – we don't need to be constantly **WORRYING** about things which can go wrong. Think of them once, prepare a solution and move on!

TEAM UP!

It's **SUPER-DIFFICULT** to hit your targets on your own.

I've already mentioned how important it is to find someone to talk about your target with, who might be able to offer you some support, advice and encouragement.

The minute we let someone help us move closer to our target, we've formed a team. It might be a team of two, or ten, or twenty – I certainly can't hit a target without help.

Teamwork can come in lots of different forms.

If you want to join a running club, then bringing a mate along for support is **TEAMWORK.**

If you want to learn the guitar, then finding someone to practise with is **TEAMWORK.**

If you want to be the world number one table tennis champion, then playing with someone else is **TEAMWORK** (it's very tough to play yourself at table tennis, trust me).

By reading this book, you've invited **ME** onto your team, to support you and give you advice and encouragement. **And I LOVE being on your team!**

REMEMBER: it's OK to ask for help. It's **MORE** than OK, it's one of the smartest things you can do! The more people you trust who know about the target you're aiming for, the more support you're going to have.

Those trusted people can also help by reminding you about your targets, by pestering you to keep working towards them, even when you're feeling a bit sluggish. And **DON'T FORGET** to give help and support back to the people on your team. One of the most satisfying things human beings can do is **help each other out.**

SMASHING IT!

Remember I mentioned how powerful your imagination is when it comes to being confident? Well, it's equally as important when we're working towards a target – **IMAGINING** what it would be like to **SMASH** that target.

What would it look like? What would it feel like? What will it sound and smell like? Once we've decided what our target is, we should always **IMAGINE** what it would be like to **SMASH** it. Then the magical power of our imagination will help bring that target closer and closer to us, just like the group of basketball players in the first chapter of this book. Remember, that group just **IMAGINED** scoring baskets and the power of their imagination helped them to do exactly that!

One of **MY** first ever **LONG-TERM TARGETS** was to perform my magic in sold-out theatres, in front of hundreds of people.

Once I had set that target, I **IMAGINED** what that would be like.

It was an incredible picture inside my head: I could see myself striding confidently on stage, I could see the illusions working perfectly, I could hear the **gasps** of the audience, the **laughter,** the **applause.** I could feel the buzz of **DOPAMINE** rushing through my body.

From those pictures inside my brain, I knew **EXACTLY** how it would feel to smash my target. And if I hadn't told myself what it would feel like, how would I have known if I had **SMASHED** my target?

I NEED A VOLUNTEER ...

Take some time to think about your targets.

TAKE AIM and think about each stepping stone you need to hop onto to smash those targets.

What **ACTIONS** do you need to take to get there?

How could you **RECORD** your progress?

How can you make a **GAME** out of your progress towards that target?

Are you **EXPECTING** any obstacles?

Who can you **TEAM** up with?

What would **SMASHING** it look like?

When you have thought through each of these questions, grab your journal, write everything down and start throwing your darts!

One of my first medium-range targets was to get my very own magic TV show on RTÉ, the national broadcaster of Ireland.

I wrote that target down in **BLACK PERMANENT MARKER** on one of the walls of my bedroom, so that I was constantly reminded of it. I wouldn't suggest doing that in your room, unless you fancy scrubbing it off with hot water while your mam or dad **ROAR** at you, but it's a good idea to write down the target and put it somewhere you'll always see it (on top of a favourite tin of biscuits perhaps!). I also wrote it down in my journal, as you should too.

Once I had **TAKEN AIM** at my target and written it down, straight away I started to take **ACTION** towards hitting it. I wrote a long explanation of what I would like the TV show to look like, then found a list of TV producers who might be able to help me to make it. I **RECORDED** my progress by ticking off every name on the list as I worked my way through it and added new show ideas to my journal.

There was another magician in Dublin at the time who was doing similar tricks to me. We had a friendly rivalry, so I made a **GAME** out of my progress by pretending that I was in a race with him to get a TV magic show on the telly. Of course, he had no idea about this imaginary race, but it helped to spur me on and work even **HARDER** to get to my target.

While I had **EXPECTED** some obstacles, the really big one came when I found that almost all of the TV producers I talked to didn't think I could do it. They didn't want to work on a TV show with me! Door after door closed in my face, which was very disheartening and tough for me. Finally, though, a producer working with Midas Productions said 'yes!', and **I TEAMED UP** with them! **Phew!**

I got a meeting with some bigwigs (as in they were important people, not people wearing big wigs. Though now I come to think of it ... **maybe** ...) at RTÉ HQ in Dublin. At that meeting, I made sure I looked as confident as possible and performed some magic for them. I got one of them to sign a playing card, which then ended up appearing stuck to the outer glass of the building we were in (always a fun trick to do).

I came out of that meeting knowing I had **SMASHED IT**, and I landed my first ever TV show: *CLOSE ENCOUNTERS WITH KEITH BARRY.*

Hitting that target meant that I could turn it into a **STEPPING STONE** towards hitting other targets.

Once I had that TV show, I was able to perform in front of hundreds of people at shows all over the country. That led to performing in America, and that then led to doing magic tricks for some **SUPER-FAMOUS** people!

I ended up outside a venue one night, very similar to the one that my mate Damien and I had tried to get into all those years ago. This time, though, I was ushered straight in and asked to perform a magic trick for a blonde woman I thought I recognised ...

Oh yeah, I thought, I **DO** recognise you!

It was the Black Widow herself, **Scarlett Johannson!**

I was a bit nervous (who wouldn't be?!) but she was lovely and chatted away happily to me. Eventually I did a trick for her where she signed a card and put it back in the deck, only to look up and see that very card stuck to the ceiling above her head! She **SCREAMED** the house down in disbelief.

Not bad for a crazy Irish magician from Waterford!

WORK BACKWARDS

Picture yourself **jumping** onto a series of stepping stones to get over a deep river. Like we've already mentioned, some targets can be used to work our way closer to bigger, long-term targets.

Take, for example, a person who wants to be fluent in Spanish before they go on holiday in six months' time.

This person could map out some stepping stones to help them on their way to that long-term target.

Maybe in one month, they will try to have learned how to **say hello** to people in Spanish, **have a simple conversation**, then **say goodbye.**

Maybe, in three months, they will try to have learned how to **say hello** to people in Spanish, **have a simple conversation,** then **say goodbye, follow directions, order food**, talk about their **favourite hobbies** and **ask lots of questions** about other people.

In six months, they will have tried to learn how to **say hello** to people in Spanish, **have a simple conversation,** then **say goodbye, follow directions, order food**, talk about their **favourite hobbies, ask lots of questions** about other people, **sing some popular Spanish songs, shop for groceries, understand football commentary** and **tell a joke** in Spanish.

These targets could be made simpler, or added to, depending on how much time the person can give to learning Spanish.

If they **RECORD** their progress properly, then they'll feel a great hit of **DOPAMINE** every time they hit a target and get that little bit closer to **SMASHING** their ultimate target.

HEY PRESTO!

1. **You won't hit your target if you don't aim at it. Clearly picture your short-, medium- and long-term targets in your mind.**

2. **When you've worked out your targets, GO AND GET THEM! Take massive action now!**

3. **Write your targets in your journal. Tick them off as you SMASH them or tweak them if you meet setbacks.**

4. **Set yourself a competition and reward yourself**

when you hit a target. Make sure your reward doesn't get in the way of hitting more targets.

5. Write down a list of problems or obstacles that might get in the way of you hitting your target. Don't WORRY about them, just PREPARE what you will do if they crop up.

6. Don't struggle to meet targets all on your own. Team up to seek help when you need it.

7. Imagine what smashing your target will look, feel and sound like. That way, you'll know when you've smashed your target.

8. Think first of your biggest target and work your way backwards to where you are now, dropping off little 'stepping stone' targets as you go.

CONJURE SOME SUCCESS!

Use your light of relaxation and breathing exercises to enter your relaxation zone.

Imagine you are out in the woods, breathing in lungfuls of cold, fresh air. Imagine your target sheet with your targets clearly printed on it. Now, imagine you are an archer, calmly loading arrows into your bow one by one and shooting them at all your targets.

See the arrows slicing through the air and thwacking into your targets each and every time.

Fire as many arrows as you need to hit each and every short-, medium-, long-term and magical target on the sheet.

*Decide on some **ACTIONS** you can take **TODAY** to move closer to those targets.*

*Now, switch the picture in your mind to what smashing your targets looks like to you. Allow the dopamine and the feeling of success to rush through your body. **Excitement! Joy! Satisfaction!***

*See yourself **SMASHING IT** and tell yourself that you are an expert archer, with the power and precision to hit your targets every time.*

Feel the happiness and the sense of satisfaction that you've got from reaching your target, whatever it might be. Your hard work and dedication has paid off!

Bring yourself back into the room that you're sitting or lying in. Begin to bring the feeling back into your toes, your legs, your whole body and then open your eyes. The moment you open your eyes, go and take one action that will help to move you closer towards your target.

CHAPTER 6

HOW MINECRAFT MAKES US MAGIC

WHAT'S THE BEST THAT CAN HAPPEN?

When we're feeling **stressed** or **anxious**, or when we end up in a difficult situation, our brains tend to bring in negative thoughts, such as 'you're not good enough'. Then we start thinking about the worst thing that could happen to us in that moment, like:

'YOU'RE GOING TO LOOK SILLY.'

OR

'YOU'RE GOING TO MESS UP – YOU'RE JUST NOT SMART ENOUGH FOR THIS.'

If we can't answer a difficult question in Irish class, we might immediately imagine ourselves failing the entire test and bringing home a sheet with a huge **FAIL** stamped on it to our parents.

If we get a bad knock on the hurling pitch and have to be taken off, we might imagine never being able to play hurling again – being stuck forever on the sidelines as our friends go on to win a county medal.

A simple trick to deal with these bad situations, when they happen, is to ask a different question.

WHAT'S THE *BEST* THAT CAN HAPPEN?

If we can pause to take a deep breath and ask ourselves that question, then we can begin to **IMAGINE** what the best outcome will be for us. Since our imagination is so magically powerful, imagining a **POSITIVE** outcome will help to calm us down and to deal with the problem that we're facing.

So, when we're facing that difficult Irish question, what's the best that can happen? You take your best guess and move on to smash every other question.

After that knock on the pitch, what's the best that can happen? You go home for a rest and wake up feeling a lot better the next day. The following week you can play again.

We should **ACCEPT** what has happened, and immediately set our **LASER-SHARP** focus on the best outcome that we can work towards.

Things go wrong **all the time.** Sometimes those can be **little things,** sometimes they can be **medium-sized things** and sometimes **big things** can go wrong.

Maybe you burnt your toast this morning.

Maybe you got the flu and missed your best mate's birthday party.

Maybe someone you loved very much passed away.

Some people ask 'why is this happening to me?' Well, it's **NOT** just you.

Bad things will happen to everyone at some stage. Like we discussed in about **TARGETS** in Chapter 5, we shouldn't spend all our time **WORRYING** about these things. We should just be prepared to deal with them when they happen.

That preparation allows us to build up our ...

RESILIENCE

Think of a suit of armour that a knight might wear before riding into battle back in medieval times. It's thick and solid, made **strong** and **sturdy** by many sheets of metal hammered together to protect the knight inside.

Resilience is just like that – we can build it up over time so that it gets **stronger** and **stronger,** and eventually it can protect us from all sorts of bad things. It's not what happens to you that matters. It's how you **REACT** to what happens to you.

I like to think about *Minecraft* when things go wrong.

Minecraft is an amazing video game that allows the player to create the most jaw-dropping buildings, civilisations and even entire planets. Players have built the Statue of Liberty, the *Titanic*, New York City, Hogwarts and countless other incredible locations from simple blocks. You might play *Minecraft* yourself in your spare time.

If you play *Minecraft*, you will know that there's always a risk that your build will be attacked and destroyed by some troublemaker. It can be **EXTREMELY** frustrating to put in hours of hard work, only to have someone come along and tear it down.

BUT!

When that happens, there is only ONE option available to us: we have to **REBUILD**.

We can't wave a magic wand and bring our beautiful build back into existence. We don't want to just turn off our computer and never play *Minecraft* again. We HAVE to rebuild, block by block. When we lay down the first block and begin to work at rebuilding our masterpiece, that is **RESILIENCE**: the magic power to **KEEP TRYING**, no matter what. That is our suit of armour, and we can make it stronger and stronger the more we practise it.

Many of the difficult moments in our lives are not always as bad as they first appear. The start of a problem is always the worst bit, so let's not hang around in that moment for too long. Begin to move forward as quickly as possible, towards accepting it and asking, **'What's the best that can happen?'**

I've had more than a few things go wrong in my own life.

But one of the biggest setbacks I've had in my life was when I was in a car crash – like a proper, full-speed, head-on **CRASH.**

I won't try to sugar-coat it: it was one of the **worst** experiences of my life. It was super-painful at the time, I got a really awful shock and, as well as that, I was told by my doctor that I would walk with a limp for the rest of my life.

That was something that was very difficult to hear. I knew right then that I would have to use **all** the brain hacks and techniques in my toolkit to move forward.

SO I DID!

I asked myself the question: **'What's the best that could happen?'** out of this terrible situation I had found myself in.

For me, the best that could happen was to be walking out on stage again, in front of a huge audience, without any hint of a limp.

I had the 'T' of my **TARGETS,** and now I had to **ACT!**

The moment I got home from hospital, I began to prepare for a BRAND-NEW MAGIC SHOW. And I was determined that I would walk onto that stage on opening night without a limp. When I told my family about my target, they thought I was **crazy.** But I had set myself a deadline, and I conjured the picture of the show in my head every day to make sure I achieved it.

Guess what! **I DID IT!**

After four months of painful treatment, exercises, tablets, and **HEAPS AND HEAPS** of hard work, I reached my target. I walked onstage to a full theatre without any limp whatsoever.

It wasn't easy. In fact, it was the exact **OPPOSITE** of easy. It took four months of gritty, hard determination to achieve. But it turned out that my suit of armour was thick enough to withstand this enormous sharp spear that had tried to puncture it. **I was resilient enough.**

With a magical mind, you can dig yourself out of **most** bad situations.

Any time you find yourself in one of those situations, ask yourself these four questions:

1. What's the best that can happen?
2. What are three things that I can do to make that thing happen?
3. Who can I ask for help?
4. Do I know anybody who has been through the same thing?

Imagine the bad situation you're in as a huge painting on the wall in front of you. Imagine pulling out your

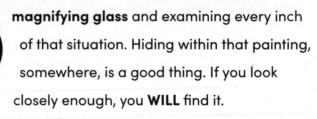 **magnifying glass** and examining every inch of that situation. Hiding within that painting, somewhere, is a good thing. If you look closely enough, you **WILL** find it.

If you look at the example of my car accident, the first good thing I found was that **I was still alive.** The next good thing was that apart from my leg, all the rest of my body parts were **still working.** The next good thing was that I was eventually able to **walk without a limp.**

So take another look at the situation and get your **magnifying glass** out. What can you see?

STEP OUT OF THAT COMFORT ZONE

So, how do we begin to **toughen up** our own personal suit of armour? How do we begin to add layers of hard steel to it so it can hold out under a stream of arrows or sudden blunt **FORCE?**

Well, we do that by stepping outside of our **comfort zone.**

We all have some kind of invisible boundary in our heads and that is our **COMFORT ZONE.** It's different for all of us, but we rarely actually realise where it is until we step out of it. Isn't that **strange?**

You might have been lucky enough to travel to a faraway place on an aeroplane, so high up in the sky it's impossible to tell when you've left one country and crossed into another. The only way you'll be able to tell is if the pilot comes on the intercom and tells you: 'We've just left Irish airspace and are now in French airspace.'

When we have moved out of our comfort zone, the 'pilot' is a **feeling** instead of a voice over an intercom. You'll know that you're outside of your comfort zone, when you're feeling **UNCOMFORTABLE.**

And who likes feeling uncomfortable? **No one.** If you've ever had a stone in your shoe, or worn a jacket that's too small, you'll know the feeling.

Joining a sports club when we don't know any of the other people there, asking an unfriendly neighbour for your ball back or telling a bully to stop what they're doing – these are all experiences that can make us feel **VERY uncomfortable.**

A lot of people dodge these uncomfortable situations like Mario dodging a bomb, but feeling that prickle of

DISCOMFORT in your brain is one of the best ways of **toughening up** your suit of armour.

If a blacksmith wants to make a suit of armour or a sword stronger, they will heat it up in their forge until it's glowing a bright red colour. Then they'll stick it in freezing cold water. This process toughens up the steel and makes sure that the blade or the armour won't shatter.

To toughen ourselves up, we need to experience both the **SEARING HEAT** and the **ICY BLAST** that being uncomfortable brings. Every time I do something uncomfortable, I feel like I am adding layers of armour around my mind, so that it will be protected when something bad happens.

Going for a dip in some freezing water (with an adult)? That's bound to make you **SUPER COLD** and **SUPER UNCOMFORTABLE** for a little while. Give it a try – scientific studies have shown that periods in cold water can boost our mood and make us feel **happier!** Another layer added!

Try a food that you think you don't like!

Try out a hobby or sport that you've never done before, ever!

Try **ANYTHING** that you find difficult or challenging and feel the layers of armour toughening up around you. These might sound like small things to do, but I **GUARANTEE** you that when life throws a bad moment at you, you will have wrapped yourself in a **THICK** suit of armour, making them easier to deal with.

I NEED A VOLUNTEER ...

Choose one of the following things to do tomorrow to make you feel **UNCOMFORTABLE:**

1. Try a food that you don't think you'll like.
2. Say sorry to someone you've had a falling out with.
3. Wash your face with icy cold water.
4. Start a conversation with a classmate you don't know very well.
5. Don't touch your favourite device for three hours.

Think of some other things that will make you uncomfortable but will also help to build up your suit of armour.

Promise yourself that you will **do something uncomfortable every day.**

Some of the most famous people in the world have had to build up their armour early in their lives, allowing them to focus even harder on reaching their **ultimate target.**

Marcus Rashford grew up in a house where his mam often struggled to pay the bills and feed her children, in an area where folks didn't have a lot of money. He's spoken about his memories of visiting food banks to get dinner on Christmas Day. He was 18 when he made his debut for **Manchester United's first team.**

J.K. Rowling received **countless** rejection letters before a publisher decided to publish the first *Harry Potter* book, but her series has now sold over **half a billion** copies worldwide.

Lionel Messi was born with a condition that meant his body didn't produce enough of the hormones needed to grow quickly enough. His family struggled to afford to pay the medical bills needed to take care of him properly. Now, he's arguably the **greatest footballer who ever lived.**

Each of these successful people had to deal with challenges and problems in their lives before they even **STARTED OUT** on the journeys that led them to where they are today. Those challenges forced them to focus on **THE BEST THAT COULD HAPPEN**, and work towards that target.

I've done the same, and **you** can too.

THE SCISSORS, THE REMOTE CONTROL AND THE PHONE

I want you to imagine standing in front of a drawer.

Pull it open and take out these **three items:**

1. **A pair of scissors.**
2. **A remote control.**
3. **A mobile phone.**

These three imaginary items are essential tools that we

can use to fight off bad experiences and have a more magical mind.

REMEMBER that it's not what happens to you that matters. It's how you **REACT** to what happens to you. **THAT** is what you can **CONTROL!** And these three items can help you.

First, let's take the scissors.

Your brain is like a hot-air balloon loaded up with supplies and equipment and kept steady by heavy sandbags hanging from its basket. You can load up your brain, just like a hot-air balloon, with all sorts of stuff – memories, emotions and information.

BUT!

You **ALSO** can dump out things that don't help you, things that weigh you down or could even send your hot-air balloon **plummeting to earth.** You can take the scissors and cut one of the ropes the sandbags are suspended from, letting it drop and leaving it far behind you.

For example, I could not tell you **ONE SINGLE FACT** about chemistry.

Isn't that **bonkers?**

I spent **YEARS** studying chemistry, even used my chemistry skills to invent a men's skincare product, and yet I now have **LITERALLY NO CLUE** about how any of it works. It's not just that I've forgotten lots of stuff, I have actually snipped the rope tying the sandbag labelled **'CHEMISTRY'** from my hot-air balloon.

Why did I do that? Because it wasn't useful to me as a magician, so my brain left it behind!

Believe it or not, **YOU** can do that too.

Not only can you snip **INFORMATION** that's weighing down your hot-air balloon, you can actually snip **BAD FEELINGS** away as well.

That doesn't mean that you will never be sad or angry or scared again – of course you will. But it won't take as long for your hot-air balloon to **RISE UP AGAIN** and head happily for the horizon.

Looking towards that horizon is a **HUGE** part of this magic trick. Focusing on the future and the best outcome that can happen will allow you to dump out those bad feelings that are weighing you down.

These feelings are part of us but are **ABSOLUTELY USELESS.** We should focus only on the things that we can control – and let the other things fall to the ground below us.

Now, let's come to the remote control ...

The old saying goes that **'time is a great healer'** – that bad things that happen to us don't hurt quite as bad as the days, weeks and months pass.

If that's true, then why don't you imagine time as a movie, or a video on YouTube? Let's get our remote control out and **FAST FORWARD** to the future, to a time when you won't feel so bad? Close your eyes and imagine what that feels like – imagine all the nerves and worry and even anger drain out of you.

REMEMBER – YOU have the remote control for your own mind and your own emotions. **YOU** are the only one who can change the channel from sadness to joy, from shyness to confidence, from anger to calmness.

Instead of **FOCUSING** on the thing that is making you feel bad, **FAST FORWARD** out of it and instead focus on the future. You can also **REWIND PAST** that bad experience or negative emotion and instead **FOCUS** on the good memories, the funny stories, the laughs and the moments of joy that you had before it.

I experienced a lot of bad feelings when my grandad passed away. Sadness, anger and grief all rushed in on top of me and tried to drag down my hot-air balloon. It tried to take over every channel in my mind, pluck the batteries out of my remote control and toss them out the window.

I knew that there was no way I was going to be able to bring my grandad back to life, so that was the first step I went through: **ACCEPTING** what had happened and working hard to **SNIP** all those negative feelings off my hot-air balloon. Remember, it's okay (and really normal) to feel sad for a long time, but I wanted to focus on the good memories of my grandad.

So I gave my remote control a good **SHAKE** and rewound the video inside my head. I rewound it back to remember all the great times we had shared together: sunny days on the beach with my grandad and my cousins, the smell of exhaust fumes from days spent watching rally races together.

It calmed me, and it helped me to think ahead, **FAST FORWARDING** to days when I would feel happier and would look back on my grandad with all the love he gave me during his lifetime.

Finally, let's take up the smartphone.

Think of your mind like the camera on a smartphone. Whenever we take a photo of something, we're making a decision about where we point the camera, how much we want to zoom in or out, whether we turn the flash on, what we focus on and who even gets to be in the photo in the first place.

When we experience something that's not very nice, or we have a bad encounter with someone, the photo that our mind chooses to take can often look **pretty ugly.**

If you miss an easy goal in the closing moments of a football match, you might see a photo of your teammates looking **angry** and frustrated as the ref blows the final whistle.

If you fail a maths test, you might get a dreary, dark image of you looking **disappointed** while your teacher looks down on you **sternly.**

JUST LIKE A SMARTPHONE, your mind has editing tools of its own!

If you spend a little time afterwards you can always edit a bad picture to make it look better.

You can crop or delete something out of the picture!

You can make it bigger, brighter and more colourful, and when it's finished you can put it in a **BEAUTIFUL** frame and hang it up over your bed!

A skyscraper looks **enormous** and **overwhelming** if you stand on the street and look up at it. But from a different view, like from an aeroplane, the skyscraper looks like one of countless other little dots on the ground far below.

HOW we look at things can make a **MASSIVE** difference to how we feel about it.

Take that photo of you having failed the maths test ... let's focus in on the mark that you actually got. **OH LOOK!** It's 5 per cent better than you got last time! You might not have passed, but your **score is improving!** Now the classroom looks bright and golden, sunlight streaming in the window, your teacher is cropped out of the image and you have a chuffed smile on your face.

Let's take another example – emptying the dishwasher.

Shudder, right?

It's a household chore that our parents often ask us to do. A lot of the time, we might feel like slumping our shoulders or rolling our eyes or groaning loudly

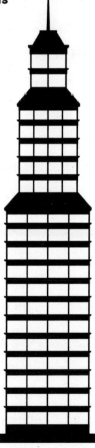

that we **HATE** emptying the dishwasher. I used to do that too!

If we say that we **'hate'** emptying the dishwasher often enough, then soon enough our brains will actually start **BELIEVING** that we hate emptying the dishwasher.

Let's try to change this picture in our head with our editing software and remind ourselves what it would be like if we **DIDN'T** have a dishwasher ...

GASP

In this situation, you might:

1. Slouch your shoulders.
2. Moan about having to wash up.
3. Argue with your siblings about whose turn it is.
4. Wrestle your siblings, and then accept defeat.
5. Pile the plates, cups, mugs and cutlery onto the counter.
6. Fill the sink with hot water and washing-up liquid.
7. Handwash each item individually.
8. Pile the clean items on the other side of the counter.

9. Dry each item with a tea-towel.

10. Put away all the items into their correct place.

Depending on the size of your family, and how ferocious your siblings are in a wrestling match, this could all take **HALF AN HOUR OR LONGER!**

That's **a lot** of time wasted every day!

So, instead of moaning about having to empty the dishwasher, we can reframe the experience by telling ourselves:

'Wow, I'm so glad we have a dishwasher. If we didn't, it would take me half an hour to get through all this. It only takes me five minutes to empty it, leaving me with **more time to play *Mario Kart*.**'

No one likes getting stuff ready for the next morning, like packing your lunchbox for school, or putting out your uniform.

But **WHAT IF** I told you that doing those things in advance means you're more organised in the morning and have an **EXTRA TEN MINUTES IN BED?**

That sounds good to me!

Bad experiences and problems will keep coming at us. Like baddies in a video game, there will **always** be another one around the corner waiting to take a swing at us.

Simply by looking at a bad experience from a different viewpoint, and **REFRAMING** it as a positive one, it will hold **MUCH** less power over us. We can then shrug it off and continue moving **FORWARD**.

HEY PRESTO!

1. **Instead of getting stuck in a terrible moment, look ahead to the BEST thing that can happen from this experience and ask yourself: 'Can we FIX it?'**

2. **Think of the best thing that can happen as a new target, and work through the TARGETS formula to SMASH IT.**

3. **Do something UNCOMFORTABLE every day, to make sure that you're constantly stepping out of your COMFORT ZONE.**

4. Delete the parts of the movie that you don't want to watch. Rewind and FAST FORWARD to the best bits.

5. Look at things from A DIFFERENT ANGLE. Very often the picture that you took can be edited and is not really as bad as you thought!

CONJURE SOME RESILIENCE!

Use your light of relaxation and breathing exercises to enter your relaxation zone.

Imagine you are looking out of a window in your house, and you notice a storm brewing. See the dark, angry-looking clouds gathering and hear the wind beginning to blow violently. Imagine this storm growing stronger and stronger as it becomes a twisting **HURRICANE!**

This hurricane is all the unexpected and unfortunate events which may happen in the future.

Now, think of someone you love who is no longer with us. It could be a friend, a relation, even a pet that you loved. I always think of my grandad for this conjuring.

Feel the warm glow of their love and energy soaking into your heart as you see them now in your mind. As you do this, gently press the index finger (the one you point with) and thumb of your hand together. Press it over and over again, like a button.

Do this for around 30 seconds as you continue to imagine your loved one's face in your mind.

By pressing your thumb and finger together, you are teaching your brain to connect that **PHYSICAL** sensation with the **BRAIN** sensation of all that love and joy brought to you by your loved one.

You are training your brain to conjure those lovely feelings whenever you press your thumb and finger together.

Allow these lovely new feelings to rush through you, gifting you the magical power to control this hurricane **NOW** and **ALWAYS.** You can now begin to shrink the hurricane, slowing the wind down and stopping the rain.

You now have control of the hurricane.

Anytime you find yourself in a difficult situation, lost in bad emotions, or being pushed to your limit, press your thumb and finger together and allow that power to flow through you again.

By practising this regularly, you will be able to magically control any storm you find yourself in.

CHAPTER 7

THE POWER OF FIVE

Having a magical mind when we go out into the real world can be **very tough.**

It's all very well to read this book, but what happens when we put the book down and it gets kicked under our bed along with all the old socks and that mouldy banana you forgot about?

Here are **FIVE** things you can do out in the real world, that will make sure you keep your mind as magical as possible.

They'll help you to feel more **confident**, **smash goals** that you've set yourself, **bounce back** when things go wrong and **be more creative** in your day-to-day life.

1. QUIET IN THE BACK!

At some point in their lives, everyone will hear a little voice of doubt in their heads telling them that they're not good enough, not talented enough, not confident enough, and lots of other nasty things.

They're like a badly behaved audience member at one of my magic shows, shouting loudly and ruining the show for everyone (including me!).

Think of that niggling little voice as a separate person and give them a name.

MOANY MICHAEL?

NEGATIVE NIAMH?

BAD MOOD BRIAN?

Name them whatever you like!

The next time you hear Negative Niamh or Bad Mood Brian start to shout at you, tell them to **BUTTON IT!**

Once the voice has shut their gob, you then need to **ARGUE BACK!** Tell them the **OPPOSITE** of what they're telling you!

If Bad Mood Brian has been shouting at you that your hair is a mess or you can't kick a football to save your life, tell him straight:

'I'M NOT TAKING FASHION ADVICE FROM YOU, BRIAN, SHUT IT!'

OR

'I'VE SCORED PLENTY OF GOALS, BRIAN, YOU OBVIOUSLY HAVEN'T BEEN COUNTING!'

If Moany Michael ever makes an appearance and says to you: 'Well, you messed that one up and embarrassed yourself,' just **SHUT HIM DOWN** and tell him: 'Enough of that, Moany Michael. I was very brave to try that and I'm proud of myself for giving it a go!'

For the next three days, in your journal write down the things that Negative Niamh or Moany Michael says to you. Do certain things come up again and again? Be extra sure to interrupt them when they bring those topics up and tell them to **CHANGE THE RECORD!**

2. HAVE A MAGICAL MORNING

Having a magical morning routine will set you up to have a magical day.

A **ROUTINE** is just a pattern that we follow over and over again.

If we always wake up late, have a rushed shower, throw on the uniform that's been lying on our bedroom floor, gulp down some breakfast and rush out the door, that's a **VERY STRESSFUL** way to start the day.

It will probably mean that we continue to feel **STRESSED, RUSHED** and even **WORRIED** as the day goes on.

Decide on a morning routine that will make you leave the house feeling **GOOD!**

Try to get up **THE SECOND** your alarm goes off, or as soon as your parents call you. It's tough at first, but making a routine of planting your feet solidly on the ground and putting one foot in front of the other is the first step to having a magical day.

Spend 15 minutes of quiet time getting some sunlight and fresh air, even by just going out in the garden or the local park and taking some deep, relaxing breaths.

Try to **AVOID** devices and telly. Instead, you could read a few pages of a comic book or newspaper or sit down with something creative that you've been working on.

Eat your breakfast slowly and carefully, paying attention to every delicious morsel that you **gobble up.**

Think carefully about the day ahead of you and **IMAGINE** the very **BEST** things that could happen today. The more you imagine them, the more confident you will be that you can conjure them into real life.

3. HIDDEN ACTS OF MAGIC

Don't keep the magic all to yourself – **spread it around**, along with some magic words!

You'll find a whole list of magic words in the next part of this book if you need some inspiration.

The idea of spreading magic is to leave **SOMEBODY OUT THERE** with a shiver of magic down their spine, an air of mystery and wonder rushing through them that could last for the entire day!

This is always a super-fun thing to do – the only rule is that with each act of magic, you must leave some unsigned **MAGIC WORDS**, so that your identity will remain a wonderful mystery!

You could ...

- Buy an elderly neighbour a little treat and leave it outside their front door, with some magic words attached.

- Plant some daffodils in random places around your neighbourhood with an adult, again with some magic words written on biodegradable wooden sticks in the ground next to them.
- Leave sticky notes with magic words written on them everywhere you go!
- Paint magic words on little rocks and leave them in random places.
- Send someone a note with some kind magic words on them, in case they need a pick-me-up!

Keep this up and you will notice how amazing you feel afterwards!

4. SAY THANKS IN YOUR JOURNAL

Make a habit out of listing in your journal **FIVE THINGS** that you are grateful for.

They don't have to be big, flashy things like a **new PlayStation** or a holiday to **Disneyland** (but if you are going, can I come in your suitcase?).

They just need to be the little things around you that make you feel good, or make you feel safe.

Start with the **really simple things:**

Be grateful for your parents or carers. For your siblings, if you have any. Be grateful for warm cups of hot chocolate. Be grateful for the rain that helps our fruit and vegetables grow! Be grateful for Smokey the cat! Be grateful for all the good memories you have! Be grateful for your grandparents, if they're still with us, and even if they're not.

List five people you can thank for helping you, no matter what they did or who they are. They could be parents, grandparents, teachers, friends, a sports coach, a dance instructor, a nice lady on the train who showed you which stop to get off at ...

Write a note in your journal explaining why you feel grateful to that person. You could even send them a note to say thanks!

5. FIND YOUR HAPPY HOBBIES

We sometimes talk about hobbies as if they're **NOT IMPORTANT.**

When I was young, getting to grips with magic for the first time, my parents described it as 'a hobby', meaning that I would have to find something a bit more **SERIOUS** to do as a career.

I tried that for a while, and then realised that my hobby was the thing that gave me more joy than anything else. And I was **GOOD** at it!

That hobby set me on a journey that would see me travel all around the world, meet amazing people, perform to huge audiences and help countless people make their life a **lot more magical.**

A **hobby** can do that!

Even if your hobby **DOESN'T** end up being your career,

it's **IMPORTANT** to have an activity that totally absorbs you. It can suck you in deeper and deeper until you can focus on only one thing: that activity. Other distractions melt away, worries or bad days dissolve into nothing. All your energy is focused on one thing, and the dopamine **rushes through you** like a high-speed train.

That's a **great** hobby.

You might have been asked at some time in your life about your 'happy place'. When people ask this, they want to know **WHERE** you feel the happiest, the place that you look forward to going more than anything else.

For you, it might be a football pitch. Or a local bookshop. Or maybe your cousins' house where you go on a Saturday to run around and make mischief.

The problem with 'happy places' is that we can only go there every now and then – they're usually spots that we don't spend much time in.

I think it's better to ask people about their 'happy hobby'. That way, we're not asking them about **WHERE** they're the happiest, but **HOW** they're the happiest.

You might be happiest with a fishing rod in your hand. Or a paintbrush. Or playing the ukelele!

Your happy hobby can be something that you do alone, or something that you do with your mates, the main thing is that it should empty your mind of **EVERYTHING** except the joy you're finding in that hobby.

Maybe you haven't found your happy hobby yet – that's not a negative, in fact, I think that's a very exciting thing to think about.

Think about all the amazing hobbies you have yet to discover! Some of them might be difficult at first, or you might have to act confidently to meet a new group of people when you start. But sooner or later you will land with a **BANG** on the one thing that makes you forget the world around you.

And that is **MAGICAL.**

CHAPTER 8

PICK A CARD...

I mentioned earlier about how powerful **MAGIC WORDS** can be to build our confidence, stretch our creativity, strengthen our resilience and help us to smash any target we set ourselves.

For this chapter, I'd like you to take a deck of cards. Remove the Jokers and lay them to one side.

You can shuffle the cards if you like – if you're not sure how, then just spread them out on a table and give them a good mix before bringing them back into a pile. Turn the pile face down.

This is now your **magic deck of cards** and will lead you towards your first set of magic words.

Pick up the top card. Once you've seen what it is, put it at the bottom of the pile.

Now, find your card in the list below. The magic words belonging to your card will be your magic words for today. Repeat them to yourself now and again, focusing intently on what they mean and how you are going to make them come true.

The more you focus on these words, the more your brain will believe them to be reality. This is a very powerful tool as you build your **magical mindset**.

Tomorrow, pick another card and repeat the process.

When you've worked your way through the deck, give them another mix and start again. The second time around, you'll be even better at **making the words come true.**

ACE OF HEARTS
'Wonderful things are coming my way.'

2 OF HEARTS
'Nothing is impossible.'

3 OF HEARTS
'All is well.'

4 OF HEARTS
'I can make a difference to the world.'

5 OF HEARTS
'There is no one in the world like me.'

6 OF HEARTS

'I can achieve anything I put my mind to.'

7 OF HEARTS

'If I need help, I can always ask for it.'

8 OF HEARTS

'I have the confidence to always be myself.'

9 OF HEARTS

'I am surrounded by people who love me and support me.'

10 OF HEARTS

'Today is going to be an AMAZING day!'

JACK OF HEARTS

'I am a good friend and I have good friends around me.'

QUEEN OF HEARTS

'I have lots of talents and abilities.'

KING OF HEARTS

'I have to be myself, because everyone else is taken.'

ACE OF DIAMONDS

'I can handle problems with resilience.'

2 OF DIAMONDS

'I am grateful for my wonderful friends and family.'

3 OF DIAMONDS

'I am proud of the things that make me different from others.'

4 OF DIAMONDS

'Today will be the start of a whole new adventure for me.'

5 OF DIAMONDS

'I can try a new challenge with courage and confidence.'

6 OF DIAMONDS

'I am a good influence on my friends.'

7 OF DIAMONDS

'I don't complain about problems – I solve them.'

8 OF DIAMONDS

'I have endless potential.'

9 OF DIAMONDS

'My creativity is just getting started.'

10 OF DIAMONDS

'I am judged not by my looks, but by what I do.'

JACK OF DIAMONDS

'I am able to forgive mistakes and move on.'

QUEEN OF DIAMONDS

'I deserve to be loved and respected.'

KING OF DIAMONDS

'My mind is magic.'

ACE OF SPADES

'I will make mistakes and learn from them.'

2 OF SPADES

'I am proud of everything I have achieved.'

3 OF SPADES

'I love being the person that I am.'

4 OF SPADES

'I can get through anything.'

5 OF SPADES

'I work hard and deserve success.'

6 OF SPADES

'I believe in myself.'

7 OF SPADES

'I am trusted by those around me.'

8 OF SPADES

'I only compare myself to the me I was yesterday.'

9 OF SPADES

'Happiness will come from inside me.'

10 OF SPADES

'Today will be an amazing day.'

JACK OF SPADES

'I am grateful for my body and all the things it can do.'

QUEEN OF SPADES

'I make other people feel happy.'

KING OF SPADES

'I am safe and surrounded by people who love me.'

ACE OF CLUBS

'I take notice of the beauty all around me.'

2 OF CLUBS

'All I can do is my absolute best.'

3 OF CLUBS

'I always see the best in people.'

4 OF CLUBS

'I deserve to have my voice heard.'

5 OF CLUBS

'I will not worry about things I cannot control.'

6 OF CLUBS

I will focus on the best thing that can happen.

7 OF CLUBS

'I will find what I love doing and do it forever.'

8 OF CLUBS

'I believe that anything is possible.'

9 OF CLUBS

'I am relaxed and I am calm.'

10 OF CLUBS

'I make the world a better place.'

JACK OF CLUBS

'All the problems I face will have solutions.'

QUEEN OF CLUBS

'Every time I face a challenge, I get stronger.'

KING OF CLUBS

'I take MASSIVE ACTION to reach my targets.'

CHAPTER 9

FUN BRAIN HACKS TO AMAZE YOUR FRIENDS AND FAMILY

These tricks are designed to make it look like you can really hack into someone's mind. When you learn the secrets to these tricks, please follow the Brain Hacker's Rules:

RULE 1: **Never** reveal the secret. (I know I am breaking this rule by writing this book!)

RULE 2: Commit to performing as if you are a real brain hacker.

RULE 3: Act the part.

RULE 4: Scripting is everything! Be sure to have a loose script to 'sell' each effect.

RULE 5: Did I mention **rule number 1**? If they really want to find out how to do the trick, tell them to buy this book!

EXTRACT A NAME FROM SOMEONE'S BRAIN!

A recording of me guiding you through this technique can be accessed on my website **www.keithbarry.com/brainhacks** (remember the password? It's **brainhacks21**).

I shouldn't be giving this away.

Seriously!

I use this all the time in impromptu situations to make it look like I'm inside someone's mind.

EFFECT:

You ask someone to think of a person they haven't thought about in a while. You hand them a slip of paper and ask them to clearly write the person's name in the centre of the piece of paper while you look away. They are instructed to fold the paper in quarters, so the name is hidden from view. You tear up the piece of paper and drop the pieces into your pocket. You then hack into their brain and reveal the name!

PROPS:

You'll need a piece of easy-to-tear paper approximately 8cm square. I often have these prepared in my wallet but, when needed, I have torn out a square from boarding passes, ticket stubs, newspapers and magazines.

SAMPLE INTRODUCTION SCRIPT:

'Did you know the brain is the world's first **supercomputer**? And just like a computer the brain can be hacked! I've just started learning how to hack into people's minds – is it okay if I try to hack your brain right now?'

METHOD:

You are going to use a technique as old as the hills called the centre tear. Draw a circle in the centre of the paper and fold it in half and then in half again, making sure the circle is on **the inside**. Show this folded piece of paper to your spectator and tell them to think of someone they haven't thought of in a while, then to open the piece of paper and print the name inside the circle. Tell them that by printing the name inside the circle they will lock that thought into their subconscious, which is what you will try to hack. Ask them to fold it back into quarters and give it back to you.

Now you will apparently tear up the piece of paper into **small pieces** in front of their eyes and tell them the name they have written down.

Here's how you do it:

- Take the folded paper back from the spectator and position it in your right hand with the folded centre positioned to your top right.
- This centre should be held between your thumb and first two fingers.
- Now tear the paper in half vertically from top to bottom.
- This will leave the centre circle undamaged, still positioned in the top right corner.
- Place the pieces from your left hand in front of the right-hand pieces and rotate everything a quarter turn to the right. The circle will now be towards you on the right-hand side, still being held by your thumb and fingers.
- Now tear the paper in half again vertically from top to bottom.
- Place the torn pieces in your left hand in front of the right-hand pieces once again.
- The torn circle will now be behind all the torn pieces facing you.
- Now drop all the torn pieces into your right-hand pocket but as you do so slide the circle back towards the middle joints of your fingers.
- Hold on to the circle.

The situation is as follows: The spectator will think you have torn up the name into shreds and dropped them into your pocket. The reality, however, is that you now have the circle, still folded into quarters, hidden in your right hand. You now need to secretly open the circle and look at the name. There are many ways to do this: If you are at a table, drop your hands naturally to your lap and open the paper. Leave it on your lap for a few moments and then take a peek at it.

If you are standing, place your hands behind your back and open the circle secretly behind your back. Keeping it hidden in your hand, you can now bring your hands forward and take the pen from the spectator. If you now hold the pen in your right hand your hand will look natural, and you can ask them to stare at the tip of the pen as you look down and look at the circle with the name on it in your left hand. As they stare at the pen, you ask them to imagine the first letter of the name hovering like a neon sign over the tip of the pen. Then begin to reveal the name, letter by letter. To clean up, simply ditch the circle in the same pocket as the torn pieces.

THE PSYCHIC ENERGY TOUCH

A recording of me guiding you through this technique can be accessed on my website **www.keithbarry.com/brainhacks** (password: **brainhacks21**).

EFFECT:

You leave the room and ask a spectator to touch any object in the room. When you are called back in, you wander around the room attempting to pick up on the psychic energy emanating from that object.

You eventually find the object, leaving everyone completely stumped.

PROPS:

A room full of objects and a secret accomplice.

SAMPLE INTRODUCTION SCRIPT:

'Did you know that by touching an object, your **energy** transfers into that object and can be still vibrating within that object for up to three hours? I've discovered I have a weird ability to pick up on that energy. Let me prove it.'

METHOD:

- This method is super simple, which allows you to focus on your acting ability to pull off the trick with **style and flair!**
- Instruct a spectator to touch any object in the room while you are outside, and the door is closed.
- Upon your return, wander around the room, touching objects at random in order to get a feel for the 'psychic energy' left behind. As you touch the objects, continuously look towards the spectator who has touched the object.
- However, what you are really doing is looking at your secret accomplice within your peripheral vision. If their feet are apart that means you are NOT touching the object. When you touch the object, your accomplice will touch their feet together.
- Once you know the object you are looking for, keep moving around touching other objects. This will put your audience off the scent. Acting is key here! Pretend you are a real psychic trying to pick up on the energy from the objects before you eventually go back and amazingly pick up

the item the spectator has touched and declare that it's the one!

- What if your accomplice is seated and you can't see their feet? No problem! They simply behave as normal as you wander the room. Again, you are looking at the spectator throughout, but also looking at your accomplice in your peripheral vision. When you touch the selected item, your accomplice will purposely not blink for a few seconds. This is almost impossible for people to spot as your accomplice knows not to stare at you! They will simply not blink for five seconds, even if they are talking to another person or apparently looking in another direction and not paying attention.

PSYCHIC CONNECTION CARD TRICK

A recording of me guiding you through this technique can be accessed on my website **www.keithbarry.com/ brainhacks** (password: **brainhacks21**).

I've been using this for years in impromptu situations as my favourite go-to card trick. It can be done anytime, anywhere, even with a borrowed deck of cards.

EFFECT:

A spectator selects a card which is then lost inside the deck. You flip through the cards and ask a spectator to merely think of the word 'STOP' when they see their card. Miraculously you find their card.

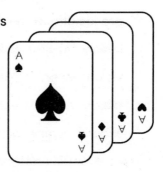

PROPS:

Deck of cards.

SAMPLE INTRODUCTION SCRIPT:

'Do you believe in **mind-to-mind communication**? Let's test my mind-reading abilities with a deck of cards.'

METHOD:

- Ask a spectator to shuffle a pack of cards. When they are finished shuffling, have them return the deck to you and take a **SNEAKY LOOK** at the card at that is on the bottom.

- You could use some imaginative scripting here to distract them from the fact that you're taking a peek at the bottom card - take the opportunity to be creative with your script!
- So you've taken a sneak peek at the bottom card, let's say it's the Queen of Spades. **REMEMBER THAT CARD**.
- Pass the pack back to the spectator and ask them to 'cut the deck', essentially to split it in half. Then you can place the bottom half on the top, but slightly askew or sideways. Distract them again by saying you are going to look away as you show them the last card in what is now the top half.
- Of course, you will know what that card is already - in this example, it's the Queen of Spades. The beauty of this trick is that no matter where the spectator splits the deck, once you place the bottom half of cards on top of the other part, you will already know what card is sitting at the bottom - and what one the spectator sees.
- Now, presentation is everything. You hold the deck face down and state, 'In a moment I will deal the cards face up onto the table. When you

see your card, please don't say anything, don't flinch, just merely think of the word '**STOP**'. I will psychically connect with you and stop at your card. Remember, please, not to say anything at all for the next 60 seconds.'

- Deal through the cards, flipping them face up one at a time. You are keeping an eye out for your key card, the card that you peeked at on the bottom of the deck earlier.

- When you see the key card, you know the next card is theirs. However, you deal past their card and continue. They will now assume you have missed it, which is exactly what we want them to think!

- Continue for about five more cards and then stop with a single card face down in your hand. State **EXACTLY** as follows: 'Would you be amazed if the next card I turned over was your chosen card?' They will be convinced you are going to turn over the card in your hand so they will agree that they would be amazed. That's when you reach down into the spread you have already dealt out and turn their card over. Watch their absolute shock when you do this. It really is a class trick which I've done weekly for the past 30 years!

- I love this trick and really want you to enjoy spreading magic and mystery in the world, so **give it a go.**

FIND THE HIDDEN OBJECT

A recording of me guiding you through this technique can be accessed on my website **www.keithbarry.com/brainhacks** (password: **brainhacks21**).

EFFECT:

You give a coin or small object to your subject and ask them to hide it in one of their hands when your back is turned. You turn your back and tell them that  once they have decided which hand to hide the coin in, they must hold that hand up to their forehead for about 10 seconds and keep thinking, 'The coin is in this hand, the coin is in this hand,' in order for them to send that thought to you and help you read their mind and body language. When they are done, they hold both hands closed into fists out in front of them. You turn around and correctly reveal which hand the coin is in.

PROPS:

A coin or something small that can be hidden in a person's hand without being seen.

SAMPLE INTRODUCTION SCRIPT:

'Do you believe I can read your mind and your body language in order to tell which hand you are hiding a coin in?'

METHOD:

- After they have held their hand to their forehead with your back turned to them for 10 seconds, ask the person to hold both arms out in front of them so both hands look identical.
- Turn back around and gaze into their eyes as if trying to hack their brain.
- Now look at their **hands**. When they place both hands out in front of you, the one that has been held up to their head will be **slightly paler** due to the lack of blood flowing to it

when it was held up against their forehead.

- Rather than select the hand straight away, however, you can play around with 'reading' their body language before revealing the correct hand.

- Now, they may say that you had a 50–50 chance of predicting the correct hand, but they will be amazed when you can do it several times in a row, even using different people. (If the results are not clear, then maybe they didn't hold their hand to their head when you turned your back.)

- Once you have done this correctly a few times, you can announce that you have now built such a good connection with the person that you don't need a coin or object anymore. You say, 'I might even be able to tell which hand you think the object is in ...' Repeat the trick without an actual object and the results will be the same as long as they hold their hand to their forehead for long enough. This will require some practice on your part, but once you get good at it, you really will feel like a real mind reader!

PRECOGNITION

A recording of me guiding you through this technique can be accessed on my website **www.keithbarry.com/brainhacks** (password: **brainhacks21**).

EFFECT:

You hand a spectator a folded piece of paper which you declare is a prediction of things to come. A spectator selects a word at random from a book as you flip through it. When they open up the prediction it says, 'On my arm.' It appears as if you have messed up the trick. You then take some coffee granules and spread them on your arm. The word the spectator is thinking of appears on your arm as if by magic!

PROPS:

A thick paperback book, a coin, some clear lip balm and some coffee granules.

SAMPLE INTRODUCTION SCRIPT:

'Have you ever heard of Nostradamus? He was a famous psychic who could apparently see into the future. I've read his book Les Prophéties and have learned to see exactly three minutes into the future. Let me show you something.'

METHOD:

- Before you begin, secretly place the coin into the book – closest to the spine, towards the front half of the book. For example, if you are using a 300-page book, then you would place the coin around page 50.

- Remember the first word at the top of the left-hand page. Let's imagine the word happens to be 'brain'. Using the lip balm, secretly write the word 'brain' big and bold on your arm. It will be completely invisible. You are now all set to perform a miracle.
- Shut the book and place it on a table, being careful of course that the coin does not fall out.
- Introduce the premise to your spectator and hand them your folded prediction, which says 'On my arm'. Next, grasp the book with the front cover facing you and the back of the book facing

the spectator. Grasp the book tightly with the spine of the book held in your left hand and you should be able to feel the coin through the pages. Now flip through the pages from back to front with your right hand and ask the spectator to call 'Stop'. As they call 'Stop', you will allow all the pages to flip by until you naturally stop at the page where there is a break from the coin.

- Try it now with this book! Grab a coin and place it at page 58 where the word 'miles' is at the top left of the page and flip through the pages as described. You will notice how easy it is to stop at the page with the coin. With practice you will be able to time this so that you naturally stop at this page the moment the spectator says 'Stop'.

- Open the book, still holding the coin through the spine, and ask them to think of the word at the top of the page in your left hand, which in our example is 'miles'. It is obvious to your spectator that you cannot see the page or word they are looking at, but to make it even more impossible, feel free to close your eyes and turn your head the other way as you open the book.

- Tell them to remember the word as you allow the book to close. Ask them to open the prediction.

This is your moment of **misdirection** to allow the coin to fall gently into one of your hands and pocket it. Don't worry – all eyes will be on the prediction. When they open the prediction, and it says, 'On my arm', you ask if it was correct. Of course, they will say you are wrong. You ask what their word was and that's when they tell you 'miles'.

- You then state, 'My prediction is actually correct – it's on my arm!' Grab a handful of coffee granules and rub them on your arm over the lip balm. The word 'miles' will reveal itself – watch them freak the freak-out of all freak-outs!

TAKE
A
BOW

Mind magic isn't a trick – it's a real thing, and it's a kind of magic that we can bring with us everywhere we go.

You can **WOW** every new person you meet with the **MAGICAL POWERS** that I've described in the pages of this book.

Now you can dive head-first into new experiences, **CONFIDENT** in your abilities to meet any challenges you face **HEAD-ON** and overcome any obstacles that come your way.

You can allow the power of your **CREATIVITY** to run **WILD**, conjuring amazing ideas and solutions out of thin air.

You can set a **TARGET** that you want to work towards, and **NEVER GIVE UP** until you achieve what you want to achieve, no matter how big or small it is.

You can pick yourself up and dust yourself off when things go wrong, using the magic power of **RESILIENCE** to **REBUILD** your confidence and your creativity.
And just like a magician's act, the possibilities are **ENDLESS**.

Like I mentioned earlier on in this book, I am **SO THRILLED** to be on your team and accompanying you on this amazing journey you're taking towards being more **MAGICAL** in everyday life.

Thank you for bringing me on this journey with you.

REMEMBER: There is no magic sprinkle, no magic dust, the real magic is inside **each and every one of you** who just took the time to read this book.

DEDICATION

Dedicated to my children, Braden and Breanna.

Braden, your ability to always pick the most expensive item on every menu inspires me to keep working hard every day. I apologise for being better at FIFA than you, but not for screaming out the window every morning when you go to school, 'Never give up' and, 'Find someone sad and make them happy'. If you read this book and absorb its contents, I predict one day you will indeed captain the Irish rugby team (but only if you eat your broccoli).

Breanna, your sense of sarcasm makes me smile every day and your daily threat to karate-kick me in the head genuinely bemuses me. While others might strive for normality, you prove time and again that embracing the quirky and unexpected is where the real fun lies. As you flip through these pages, remember that life's greatest tricks often involve embracing your inner weirdo.

Here's to both of you – amazing human beings who defy the norm with your quirky personalities.

And to your mum, Mairead, who wholeheartedly embraces the wonderfully strange journey we're all on together and keeps us all somewhat grounded with her unwavering support and endless patience.

ACKNOWLEDGMENTS

I would like to thank Venetia, Sarah, Aoife, Mia and all in Gill Books for all their support, guidance and help in creating the book that's now in your hands.

Thanks to Nick for the endless late nights spent putting my thoughts onto paper.

Thanks to Michele and Alanna for picking thousands of cards over the years; to Al for your endless curiosity and support; to Rhona, Ian and Marie for endless laughs; to Sean for your level head in tough times and to Bart for listening to all of my crazy ideas over the years.

Thanks to Jose for being my invisible ninja for all these years; to Joe for locking yourself in a cabin with me for eighteen months; to Colly for being 'positronic' through thick and thin.

To Tony Sadar for your amazing wisdom; Doc Shiels for your mysterious ways; and Ann and Declan for putting up with my madness!

Above all, thanks to my amazing parents, Ken and Kitty, for a life filled with magic.

JOURNAL NOTES

For permission to reproduce illustrations, the author and publisher gratefully acknowledge the following:

© Adobe Stock: 65, 68, 98, 101, 105, 115, 116, 151, 152, 156, 175; © Freepik: 36, 44, 75, 77, 97, 109, 140, 157, 192; © Shutterstock/ mijatmijatovic: 131; © Shutterstock/ Natchapol18: 139.

The author and publisher have made every effort to trace all copyright holders, but if any have been inadvertently overlooked we would be pleased to make the necessary arrangement at the first opportunity.